Ancient Fragments, Containing What Remains of the Writings of Sanchoniatho, Berossus, Abydenus, Megasthenes, and Manetho

THE

ANCIENT FRAGMENTS;

CONTAINING

WHAT REMAINS OF THE WRITINGS OF

SANCHONIATHO, BEROSSUS, ABYDENUS,
MEGASTHENES, AND MANETHO.

ALSO

THE HERMETIC CREED, THE OLD CHRONICLE,
THE LATERCULUS OF ERATOSTHENES,
THE TYRIAN ANNALS,
THE ORACLES OF ZOROASTER,
AND THE PERIPLUS OF HANNO.

BY I. P. CORY, ESQ.
FELLOW OF CAIUS COLLEGE, CAMBRIDGE.

LONDON:
WILLIAM PICKERING.
MDCCCXXVIII.

PREFACE.

In presenting this collection of ANCIENT FRAG-
MENTS to the world, some explanation of what is
comprehended under that title is not altogether
unnecessary. We are accustomed to regard the
Hebrew scriptures, and the Greek and Latin
writings, as the only certain records of antiquity:
yet there have been other languages, in which
have been written the annals and the histories of
other countries. Where then are those of Assyria
and Babylon, of Persia and Egypt and Phœnicia,
of Tyre and Carthage? Of the literature of all
these mighty empires where are even the remains?
It will, no doubt, tend to excite some reflections of
a melancholy cast, to look on this small volume as
an answer. That they are all contained in it, I
should be unwilling to assert: yet, with some dili-
gence and research, I have not been able to dis-
cover other fragments, which I could consider
sufficiently authenticated, to increase its size.

It was my wish to have included in this collection all the fragments of the earlier Gentile world,
which have reached us through the medium of the

b

Greek language. Of the early historians of Greece the names only of some have come down to us; whilst of others, such as Eupolemus and Histiæus, several very interesting fragments have escaped the general wreck. In the classic ages of their literature, the acquaintance of the Greek historians with antiquity is generally confined and obscure: nor was it till the publication of the Septuagint, that they turned their attention to the antiquities of their own and the surrounding nations and for this reason we meet with more certain notices of ancient history in the later, than in the earlier times of Greece. To have drawn a line then, to have inserted the earlier writers to the exclusion of the later, would have been to omit the more valuable. To have reprinted the fragments of many authors, such as Nicolaus Damascenus, a writer of Damascus, of the Augustan age, would have introduced, with some matter worthy of attention, much of little interest. To have selected from them all, the passages relating to ancient times and foreign states, would have been a task as useless as laborious, and would have swelled the collection to a series of volumes. I have therefore excluded all native Greek historians—and every writer of the Augustan age and downwards—I have also omitted all fragments which bear about them the stamp of forgery, or are the productions of Hellenistic Jews; or of authors who have had access to the sacred Scriptures, and following the words throw no additional light upon the subjects under one or other of which divisions may be classed the Antediluvian books of Enoch, the large fragments of Artapanus, the Sibylline Oracles, the correspondence of Solomon and Hiram king of Tyre, the tragedy of Ezekiel in which Moses figures as the hero, with several compositions of a similar description.

The contents then of this volume are Fragments which have been translated from foreign languages into Greek; or have been quoted or transcribed by Greeks from foreign authors; or have been written in the Greek language by foreigners who have had access to the archives of their own respective countries. They are arranged under the following heads: the Phœnician, the Chaldæan, the Egyptian, the Tyrian, the Persian, and the Carthaginian.

In the following review of these ancient writers, I have passed from themselves into a slight examination of their works: not with a view of entering at all into the details, but merely to call the attention to some few great landmarks, which stand prominently forth amidst what might otherwise be deemed a wild, pathless and interminable. For the most ample and satisfactory explanation of the whole, I must refer to the inimitable works of Mr. Faber and Bryant.

Under the first head is contained only the Phœnician Theology of Sanchoniatho, who is considered to be the most ancient writer of the heathen world. In what age he wrote is uncertain : but his history was composed in the Phœnician language, and its materials collected from the archives of the Phœnician cities. It was translated into Greek by Philo Byblius, and for the preservation of these fragments we are indebted to the care of Eusebius. I have deviated but little from the quaint translation of Bishop Cumberland, generally so far only as to render it more consonant with the text of Stephen, or to substitute more modern expressions for phrases become now almost obsolete.

The cosmogony is one of those jargons of Theology and Physics, which were refined by the later heathens into some resemblance of the sublimest mystery of the Christian faith. As the most ancient, it is the most valuable ; and as it speaks more plainly than the rest, it affords a key to their interpretation

The generations contain many very curious passages. They are the only well authenticated heathen account of the times before the flood

In the first generation is an allusion to the fall : in the second Genus may be Cain : after which we lose the traces of similarity : at the fifth there is an interruption. But taking up the thread of inquiry, at the end of the first line, in Taautus or Thoyth, we may perhaps recognize Athothis, the second king of Egypt, the Hermes Trismegistus, who appears again as the adviser of Cronus. His predecessor Misor, corresponds then with Mizraim, the first king of Egypt, the Menes and Mines of the dynasties. In the preceding generation is Amynus, Ammon, or Ham, the same with the Cronus, of what is supposed a different line. An ascent higher we find, Agrus, the husbandman, who was worshipped in Phœnicia as the greatest of the gods: he corresponds with Noah, the Ouranus of the other line, whose original name was Epigeus or Autochthon, a name of similar import with Agrus. There is also some slight appearance of identity between Hypsistus, the father of Autochthon or Ouranus, and Geinus Autochthon, the father of Agrus.

The generations conclude with an intimation, that they contain the real history of those early times, stripped of the fictions and allegories with which it had been obscured by the son of Thabion, the first hierophant of Phœnicia. That such is the case we are assured by Philo Byblius, in the remarks on Sanchoniatho with which he prefaces his translation of the work. The passage also informs us that the history thus disguised was handed down to Isiris, the brother of Chna, the first Phœnician. Bishop Cumberland conjectures that this Isiris is the Osiris of the Egyptian worship, and with greater probability supposes him the same with Mizraim, the son of Ham, who was the brother of Canaan. But he strangely wanders from the truth in his researches after the son of Thabion. If the legends were handed down to Isiris, the son of Ham, they must have been handed down by one of the predecessors of this Isiris, that is by Noah, or one of his own sons· Thabion is derived from Theba the Ark, and in the phraseology of Bryant is equivalent to the Arkite: it is a title of Noah· therefore the first hierophant of Phœnicia was a son of Noah, a predecessor of Mizraim and Canaan, an inhabitant also of Phœnicia, in short was Ham himself And it is some confirmation, indirect enough it must be owned, of the very prevalent belief in the apostacy of that patriarch.

This fragment is succeeded by a stricture on the propensity of the Greeks for allegory. Several of these strictures occur in the course of the extract. I have generally omitted them as they appear to be the words of Philo, the translator, and could never have been those of so early a writer as Sanchoniatho. But to exhibit the argument in the adverse light, it may be urged, that since these strictures on the Greeks occur, Sanchoniatho could not have written in such ancient times Be that as it may, the passages have no connection with the history, and at any rate were not contained in the Phœnician records.

The last fragment, upon the mystical sacrifice of the Phœnicians, is so singular, that I cannot forbear inserting the conclusion of Bryant's dissertation on the subject. After having shewn that this is the only sacrifice among the ancients, which is termed *mystical;* and that Cronus, the personage who offers it was the chief deity of the Phœnicians; and moreover, that it could not relate to any previous transaction, he concludes thus:—

" The mystical sacrifice of the Phœnicians had these requisites, that a *prince was to offer it;* and *his only son was to be the victim:* and as I have shewn that this could not relate to any thing *prior;* let us consider what is said upon the subject, as *future,* and attend to the consequence. For if the sacrifice of the *Phœnicians* was a type of *another* to come; the nature of this last will be known from the representation, by which it was prefigured. According to this, *El,* the supreme deity, whose associates were the Elohim,* was in process of time to have a son, αγαπητον well-beloved: μουνγενης, his only begotten: who was to be conceived (of αναβρεσ), as some render it, of *grace:* but according to my interpretation, of *the fountain of light.* He was to be called *Jeoud* whatever that name may relate to ; and to be *offered up as a sacrifice to his father* λυτρον, by way of *satisfaction,* and *redemption,* τιμωραις δαιμοσι, *to atone for the sins of others,* and *avert the just vengeance of God;* αντι της παντων φθορας, to prevent universal corruption, and at the same time, *general ruin.* And it is farther remarkable ; *he was to make*

* See page 11.

the grand sacrifice βασιλικω σχηματι κενοσμηρμενος, *invested with the emblems of royalty.* These surely are very strong expressions: and the whole is an aggregate of circumstances highly significant, which *cannot be the result of chance.* All, that I have requested to be allowed me in the process of this recital, is this simple supposition, that *this mystical sacrifice was a type of something to come:* how truly it corresponds to that, which I imagine it alludes to, I submit to the reader's judgment. I think, it must be necessarily esteemed a most wonderful piece of history."

Sanchoniatho wrote also a history of the serpent. A single fragment of which is preserved by Eusebius.

The Chaldæan Fragments are chiefly from Berossus and Megasthenes

Berossus, a Babylonian, flourished in the reign of Alexander, and lived some time at Athens: and according to many wrote his Chaldæan history in the Greek language. As a priest of Belus he possessed every advantage, which the records of the temple and the learning and traditions of the Chaldæans could afford; and seems to have composed his work with a serious regard for truth. He has sketched his history of the earlier times from the representations on the walls of the temples: from written records and traditionary knowledge, he learned several points too well authenticated to be called in question; and correcting the one by the other has produced the strange history before us.

The first fragment, a catalogue of the Chaldæan Kings, has been preserved by Apollodorus; and the second, another version of the same with an epitome of the account of the deluge, by Abydenus, a disciple of Aristotle. The large extract preserved by Alexander Polyhistor, is extremely valuable; and contains a store of very curious information.

The first book of the history opens naturally enough with a description of Babylonia. Then referring to the paintings, the author finds the first series a kind of preface to the rest. All men of every nation appear assembled in Chaldæa: among them is introduced a character, who is represented as their instructor in the arts and sciences, and informing them of the events, which had previously taken place. Unconscious that Noah is represented under the character of Oannes, Berossus describes him, from the hieroglyphical delineation, as a being literally compounded of a fish and man, and as passing the natural, instead of the diluvian, night in the sea, with other circumstances indicative of his character and life.

The instructions of the Patriarch are detailed in the next series of paintings. In the first of which, I conceive, the Chaos is portrayed by the confusion of the limbs of every kind of animal: the second represents the creation of the universe: the third the formation of mankind: others again that of animals, and of the heavenly bodies.

The second book appears to have comprehended the history of the ante-diluvian world: and in this the two first fragments ought to have been inserted The historian seems to have confounded the history of the world with that of Chaldæa. He finds nine persons, probably represented as kings, preceding Noah, who is here again introduced under the name of Xisuthrus, and supposes that the representation was of the first dynasty of the Chaldæan kings. From the universal consent of history and tradition he was well assured that Alorus or Orion, the Nimrod of the Scriptures, was the founder of Babylon and the first king· consequently he places him at the top, and Xisuthrus follows as the tenth. The destruction of the records by Nabonnasar left him to fill up the intermediate names as he could : and who are inserted, is not so easy to determine. If they are the predecessors of Noah; who are the Annedoti that appear to them? or can these appearances relate to any ante-diluvian transactions of the Patriarch ? If they are the successors of Nimrod, the appearances of the Annedoti may refer to visits of the Patriarch and his sons: yet every remnant of the heathen accounts, which in anywise relates to this subject, affirms the violent destruction of the tower of Babel, the dispersion of its builders, and the long subsequent desolation of the city.

There is, however, a dynasty of Chaldæan kings, handed down as some suppose by Berossus, of which the following is a list of the names.

1.	Ευηχοος	Evechous	6 Years
2.	Χομασβολος	Chomasbolus	7 Years.
3.	Πωρος	Porus	35 Years.
4	Νεχωβης	Nechobes	43 Years
5.	Αβιος	Abius	45 Years.
6.	Ονιβαλλος	Oniballus	40 Years
7	Ζινζιρος	Zinzirus	45 Years.

These Mr. Faber conjectures to have been the immediate descendants and successors of Nimrod in Nineveh, the new seat of his empire after the catastrophe at Babylon; and that the long continuation of Assyrian monarchs are the descendants of the same patriarch but of a younger branch. Bryant fancies he recognizes among them the predecessors of Nimrod, and thinks the list altogether spurious.

There is also a dynasty of Arabian kings of Chaldæa, who seem to have taken possession of Babylon during the long period of its desolation, and to have reigned there independent of the Assyrian empire. They were six in number, five of whose names are preserved.

1.	Μαρδοκεντης	Mardocentes	45 Years
2.	Σισιμαδακος	Sisimadacus	28 Years.
3.	Γαβιος	Gabius	37 Years.
4	Παραννος	Parannus	40 Years.
5.	Ναβοννοβος	Nabonnabus	25 Years
6	. . . .	.	41 Years.

They are to be found in Syncellus.

The history of the flood is very interesting, and wonderfully consonant with the Mosaic account. It mentions also the circuitous route of the human race from Armenia to the plains of Shinar.

The fragment on the Tower of Babel is generally quoted as from Abydenus. Whether it is part of his own work, the Assyrian history, or was extracted by him from Berossus, or transcribed from the Scriptures is extremely questionable: indeed it has much the air of a forgery.

The small fragment (page 32) is supposed by Eusebius, who quotes it, to relate to Abraham. Nor is this improbable: a similar passage is found in Nicolaus Damascenus, which mentions the patriarch by name, and styles him King of Damascus, a title which is given him by other writers.

The other fragments of Berossus are well authenticated history, and throw some light upon the scriptural account of the same persons and transactions. It may be observed that Belshazzar, represented in Daniel, as the son of Nebuchadnezzar, is Neriglissoor, who married the daughter, and afterwards conspired against and slew the son of that monarch; succeeded to the kingdom; and was himself taken off by violence. Nabonnedus corresponds with Darius the Mede, who afterwards took the kingdom, and was conquered by Cyrus.

The last fragment is from Megasthenes, a Persian, who wrote an Indian history a few years subsequently to Berossus. The prophecy of Nebu-

chadnezzar apparently alludes to some public noti-
fication of Daniel's interpretation of his dream.
The Mede he mentions may be Nabonnedus, the
Darius of the Scripture.

The singular creed, which stands first of
the Egyptian fragments, was transcribed by Jamblichus, from the Hermetic books It is an
exposition of that first principle of the heathen
theology, which, with its hypostases, was so largely,
insisted upon by the school of Plato; and, according to them, so continually passed over in silent
reverence by the earliest heathens.

I have retained the translation of Jones of
Nayland, from his Philosophical Disquisitions; and
which may be found also in his answer to the
Essay on Spirit: and I may refer to those works
for the most intelligible and satisfactory exposition
of this, and of the other heathen trinities.

Previously to the dispersion at Babel, the apos-
tates from the primitive worship were divided into
two sects, whose religion Mr. Faber commonly dis-
tinguishes by the titles of Buddhism and Brahmenism. They differed not so much in the original
objects of their adoration, as in their form of worship. While the latter descended to the introduction of images, and diverged with every kind of
polytheistical absurdity; the former stopped content
with a more simple scheme of theology; and in
some countries, such as Persia, an almost pure Sa-
bianism was jealously preserved. Both were widely

diffused and often, as in Egypt and Greece, amalgamated into one. The more elaborate and corrupted system of Brahmenism would catch the attention of the casual observer as the religion of the land; while the deeper doctrines, which involved much of the Buddhic theology, were wrapped in mystery, and communicated only to the initiated.

That the heathen trinities are often variations of the Patriarchs, the Divi of the ancient worship, who were canonized under the titles of Ouranus, Cronus, Jupiter, &c. combined with the ark and other symbols, is demonstrated by Mr. Faber and others, too clearly to admit of doubt: yet, still more frequently, when stripped of their theological dress, will they resolve themselves into some mere physical principle of nature, or its poweis: of which the piesent collection affoids other decisive instances both in Sanchoniatho and Zoroaster. Among the ancient heathens the Chaos was an object of veneration; it was looked upon as the first gieat principle, and usually occupies the first place, in those creeds which bear a trinitarian aspect. The other persons of the Triad are equally material: the second is frequently the Sun, or the Light, or rather Ether, the Soul of the World, or the great Patriarch himself: and the third, the Host of Heaven, the Stars, the Soul of the World, or the conseciated Dæmons. There was a foundation of Materialism, on which was raised a superstructure of Idolatry.

In the classic ages of Greece and Rome appeared a race of philosophers, who, while they submitted to superstitions which they sometimes scorned, must be allowed to have lifted up their minds to truth, as high as unassisted reason might avail. A Christian may despise, as rank idolatry, the weakness or hypocrisy, which could bow down before the images, and pray to the departed spirits of their patriarchal Divi, either as agents or intercessors; but he must admit that their aspirations towards the first great cause soared far above materialism, and were wholly directed to a sublimer object of veneration. By them the ancient creeds were made to speak a loftier language, which was foreign to their original import; and upon the promulgation of Christianity they were again remodelled and refined into a further resemblance of its mysteries And such has probably been the fate of the Hermetic creed before us.

The old Egyptian Chronicle, preserved by Syncellus, is a valuable guide and index to the dynasties that follow.

The first fragment of Manetho, his Epistle to Ptolemy Philadelphus, king of Egypt, gives an account of the author and his work. His history was composed by order of that king in emulation of the Septuagint · and its materials collected, under the royal command, from all the records of the kingdom. All that remains is an epitome of the dynasties, and two large extracts; the first concerning the Shepherd kings, and the other upon the Israelites.

In the dynasties I have followed the text of Africanus, as quoted by Syncellus, in preference to that of Eusebius who has sadly defaced it. The general outline is the same, though the names of the kings, and the length of their respective reigns frequently differ, as well as the collocation and numbers of the dynasties. I have availed myself of the text of Eusebius to correct grammatical errors ; but where any material difference occurs, I have inserted the variation in a parenthesis, or observed it in a note. The numerical letters or figures I have given from Africanus without noticing those of Eusebius as very little dependence can be placed on either.

The Laterculus or Canon of the Kings of Thebes was compiled from the archives of that city by Eratosthenes, the librarian to Ptolemy Philadelphus. It is to be found in Syncellus and other writers.

From these fragments, as explained by the ingenious dissertations of Bryant and Mr. Faber, we may collect an outline of the early history of Egypt. It appears then that after the dispersion from Babel the children of Mizraim went off to Egypt ; of which they continued in the undisturbed enjoyment for about two centuries and a half. The first fourteen dynasties have given rise to various hypotheses. Bryant, using the Old Chronicle as an authority, lops them all off at once as spurious. There is nevertheless great reason to suppose that the first, or at least part of it, is genuine. Menes, Mines, or Mizor, the Mizraim of the Scriptures, and the planter of the nation, is naturally placed as the first sovereign of the united realm : and perhaps the dominion of Athothis was equally extensive; for his name occurs both in the Laterculus of the Theban Kings, and in Sanchoniatho. After him the country seems to have been divided into several independent monarchies; some of whose princes may perhaps be found among the thirteen dynasties that follow.

The first fragment from Josephus, gives an account of the invasion and expulsion of a race of foreigners, who were styled Hycsos or Shepherd Kings. They were a branch of the warlike family of the Cuthites, who took advantage of the divided state of Egypt, and conquered it with little difficulty. They retained possession for nearly two hundred and sixty years; when they were expelled by a combination of the native princes under Thummosis, king of Thebes. The Shepherds are placed as the fifteenth dynasty, and Thummosis and his successors, correspond accurately with Amos the first king and his successors of the eighteenth dynasty. Very shortly after the expulsion of the shepherds, Joseph and the children of Israel, came down into Egypt, and were settled in the land of Goshen, he Avaris, which had been evacuated by the Shep-

herds; where they seem to have lived more than a
century on terms of the greatest amity with the
Egyptians, till a second invasion of the Shepherds
reduced them to a state of slavery. Of this invasion the second extract gives an account, and
places it in the reign of Amenophis, whom the
historian identifies with Amenophis the third, by
making him the predecessor of Sethos his son, whom
we find the first of the nineteenth dynasty, and
who was named Ramesses, after Rampses the father
of Amenophis. According to the fragment, the
Shepherds effected the conquest in alliance with
the Israelites, with whom they reigned conjointly
thirteen years, during which time Amenophis,
with multitudes of his subjects, retired into Ethiopia By a comparison of the fragment with the
Mosaic account, and some passages relative to the
same transactions in Diodorus, Herodotus, and Ta-
citus, Mr. Faber has extracted the following particulars; that instead of thirteen years, one hundred
and six must be allotted to the duration of the
second shepherd dynasty; the five hundred and
eleven years mentioned by Manetho, being the
complete interval between the first invasion and
final expulsion: that the native Egyptians and
Israelites were equally oppressed under their sway:
that the Pyramids were constructed by the joint
labours of the conquered, at the command of
Cheops, one of the Shepherd kings: and that the
Exodus of the Israelites, and destruction of the

Shepherd's power were effected at the same time, by the passage of the Red Sea. After the power of the Shepherds was broken by that catastrophe, the native princes returned, and seem to have had some difficulty in expelling the remnant of the Shepherd tribe; which was finally effected by Sethosis, in the emigration of the Danai to Greece.

The second invasion then must have taken place in the reign of Amenophis the second ; and the return of the Egyptian kings from Ethiopia, in the person of Amenophis the third, who has been confounded with his predecessor. The kings of the second dynasty of Shepherds, seem to have been but two, Cheops and Chephren according to Herodotus, the Chemmis and Cephren of Diodorus. They correspond apparently with Suphis, and Suphis the second which are placed in the fourth of the dynasties of Manetho The second dynasty of Shepherds, was in reality the fourth dynasty of Egypt, which is expressly stated to have been Memphites of a different race : and of these Suphis the first is said by Africanus, to be the same as Cheops. By turning also to the Laterculus we may observe, at the fifteenth, a change of dynasty from Theban Egyptian to Theban kings : and in Saophis and Sensaophis or rather Saophis the second, we may recognise the same persons reigning as the kings of Thebes. The Mencheres of Manetho, who follows Suphis, is probably the Mycerinus of Dio-

dorus and Herodotus, and the Moscheris of Eratosthenes; and a similarity in the names of his
successors to those of the successors of Acherres*
in the eighteenth, may induce us to suppose they
were the same persons, the exiled princes of Egypt,
the contemporaries and not the successors of the
second race of Shepherd kings. If any reliance
may be placed upon the numbers, another argument
might be drawn from the sum of the united reigns
which amounts in all the three cases to something
more than a century. For a very ingenious theory,
I may also refer to the Egyptian Mythology of
Pritchard, in which he separates the Theban,
Memphite, Thinite, Elephantine, Xoite, and Heracleotic dynasties from each other, and looks upon
them as independent and often contemporaneous
dynasties.

The Tyrian Annals are fragments, which were
quoted by Josephus from the now extinct histories
of Dius and Menander. They agree perfectly with
the scriptural accounts, and furnish some curious
particulars in addition. The date of the foundation of Carthage, it may be observed is accurately
fixed.

The fragments of Zoroaster are generally known

* Possibly the name was Cheres or Ares, varied by the common prefixes of Men, Ach, &c

by the title of the Chaldaic Oracle of Zoroaster.
A few of them were first published by Ludovicus
Tiletanus at Paris, with the commentaries of
Pletho ; to which were subsequently added those of
Psellus The rest were collected by Franciscus
Patricius from the works of Proclus, Hermias, Sim-
plicius, Damascius, Synesius, Olympiodorus, Nicephorus, and Arnobius ; and published together with
the Hermetic Books at the end of his Nova Philo-
sophia. Stanley in his lives of the Philosophers, has
given the complete collection of the oracles, with a
translation into English, to which I have generally
adhered.

Great doubts have been entertained respecting
the authenticity of these oracles: but the variety of
authors by whom they have been quoted, and
throughout whose works they lie dispersed, speaks
something in their favour. That they were the
forgery of some Gnostic, is an opinion which Stanley thinks sufficiently refuted by the great veneration in which they were held by the Platonic
school.

The oracles of Zoroaster, if not genuine extracts,
at least contain the genuine doctrine of the Sabæan
Theology The writings which are extant under
the title of the Hermetic books though of a far
more suspicious character, and evidently the compositions of a later age, have by several eminent
writers been also supposed to contain the real doctrines of the Egyptian Buddhists. Both savour per-

haps too strongly of the Platonic philosophy : but that peculiar phraseology, by which the materiality of their subject is sublimated into a spiritual form, must be attributed to the Greek translators, who had deeply imbibed the doctrines of that school.

The Periplus of Hanno is an account of the earliest voyage of discovery extant. It was taken from an original and apparently official document which was suspended in the temple of Saturn, at Carthage. Mr. Falconer has edited it as a separate work, and gives two dissertations on it; the first, explanatory of its contents; and the second, a refutation of Mr. Dodwell's reflections on its authenticity. I have followed Mr. Falconer both in his text and translation. With respect to its age, Mr Falconer agrees with Bougainville in referring it to the sixth century before the Christian era.

The Periplus is prefaced by a few lines, reciting a decree of the Carthaginians relative to the voyage and its objects : and is then continued as a narrative, by the commander or one of his companions, which commences from the time the fleet had cleared the straits of Gibraltar. Mr. Bougainville has given a chart of the voyage, which may be found, together with the corresponding maps of Ptolemy and D'Anville, in Mr. Falconer's treatise. It may be sufficient however, to remark that Thymiaterium, the first of the colonies planted by Hanno, occupies a position very nearly, perhaps precisely the same with that of the present com-

mercial city of Mogadore. The promontory of Soloeis corresponds with Cape Bojador, nearly opposite to the Canaries. Caicontichos, Gytte, Acra,
Melitta and Arambys are placed between Cape
Bojador and the Rio d'Ouro which is supposed to
be the Lixus. Ceine is laid down as the island of
Arguin under the southern Cape Blanco : the river
Chretes perhaps is the St. John, and the next large
river mentioned is the Senegal. Cape Palmas and
Cape Three Points, are supposed to correspond
respectively with the Western and Southern Horns,
and some island in the Bight of Benin, with that of
the Gorillæ. Vossius however supposes the Western Horn, to be Cape Verd, and the Southern,
Cape Palmas, in which case the Sierra Leone will
answer to the Ochema Theon the Chariot of the
Gods.

The description of the Troglodytæ, as men
of a different form or appearance, may imply
a change from the Moresco to the Negro race.
Some passages, quoted by Mr. Falconer from Bruce's
travels, explain the extraordinary fires and nightly
merriment, which alarmed the voyagers, as customs
common among many of the negro tribes, and
which had repeatedly fallen within the scope of
his own observations. The Gorillæ are supposed
to be large monkeys or wild men as the name
ανθρωποι αγριοι may in fact import.

It is needless to take notice of the numerous

forgeries, which have been issued as the productions of the authors of these fragments. There is
a complete set which was composed in Latin by
Annius, a monk of Viterbo. But it is a singular
circumstance, and one which might be urged with
great force against the genuineness of almost the
whole collection, that not only the original authors
have perished, but those also, through whose means
these relics have been handed down. With the
exception of these fragments, not only have Sanchoniatho, Berossus, and the rest passed on into
oblivion ; but the preservers of their names have
followed in the same track, and to a more unusual
fate. The fragments of Philo, Abydenus, Polyhistor, Dius, and the others, are generally not those
of their own works, but extracts from their predecessors.

It is necessary also to advert to the numerous
errors which will be found in every sheet. The
fragments have been exposed to more than the
common risks, and accidents, to which all ancient
writings have been subject. They have been
either copied from the rude annals of antiquity, or
sketched from historical paintings or hieroglyphical
records, they have been sometimes translated from
the sacred, into the common language of the place,
and again translated into Greek ; then passed in
quotation from hand to hand, and are now scattered
over the works of the fathers, and the writers of
the Roman empire. It is matter of surprise then,

not that they abound in error and uncertainty, but that so much has been preserved. For my own errors and inadvertencies I beg leave humbly to apologise, yet I must confess I have some reason to congratulate myself on finding in the above a cloak, under which a multitude of them may be con‐ cealed, and to which a charitable disposition may refer as many as it pleases without even recurring to the " errors of the press."

Several of these fragments are preserved in two or three different authors, each of whom con‐ tains a different version of the same, differing not so much in the outline, and in the general flow of words, as in those technicalities and variations of termination which were necessary to adapt them to the author's style, and it has been a source of some little perplexity to determine which of these various readings to prefer.

To Eusebius, Syncellus, and Josephus, we are principally indebted for these relics of antiquity. The authors of them are repeatedly cited in the Stro‐ mata of Clemens Alexandrinus, and in the works of Justin, Cedrenus, and the fathers of the lower empire : but unfortunately no extracts have been preserved. Diodorus Siculus has borrowed largely, but has incorporated the substance of his quotations in the body of his own work.

For Josephus I have followed Hudson's edition The Cologne edition of the Præparatio Evangelica

e

of Eusebius is often considered as the best: but upon close inspection and comparison I have been induced to prefer the text of Stephen. With the exception of a mutilated translation into Latin, Eusebius' Chronicle is lost. Under that title however Scaliger has industriously compiled a very portly folio, which, with some other Chronicles, contains a collection of all the fragments of the Greek text of Eusebius, that could be found. Syncellus has been magnificently edited at Paris under the patronage of Louis the fourteenth. By that father very copious extracts have been preserved. He professes to follow the original documents more closely that his predecessors, and as his Parisian editor makes the same pretences to fidelity, I have very generally taken his text as the groundwork. To correct all the palpable grammatical errors contained in it, would be a difficult undertaking· To effect it in some degree, I have availed myself of the emendations of the margin, and of the different readings to be found in Eusebius. But in no case have I presumed to alter without authority; and where neither the margin nor Eusebius afforded that, I have permitted the error to stand as I found it The alteration of a single letter would sometimes correct a gross grammatical mistake: yet at the same time by retaining the letters as they stand, and making a different division of them into words, a different meaning may be elicited. This work being a mere collection of quotations,

I have not deviated from the usual method of quoting without the points. In most cases we make no use of them : in some instances, their introduction might stamp one particular signification upon certain passages, in which two, widely different, present themselves : but where so much uncertainty prevails, every person must be at liberty to accent as he pleases, or to divide the words as best may suit his purpose. To introduce the accents generally, and omit them in those sentences which may bear a double import, and in which they might assist us to determine the meaning; in short, to use them where they are of no use, and omit them where they might be turned to some account, would be an eccentricity, more needing an apology, than the course I have ventured to pursue. The matter contained in these fragments is the only merit to which they can pretend; the interpretation is all that is required; and refined criticism, bestowed on works which do not rise to elegance, is always a misplaced display of learning : and I feel myself as little competent as inclined to enter into speculations upon the words or accents. So far from presuming to intrude into the province of a commentator, I shall be well content if I have committed no great mistakes.

Such as these fragments are, I send them forth without either note or comment. The classical reader will find, I fear, but poor amusement in perusing a half barbarous dialect, replete with errors and inconsistencies: to the student of divinity, however, they may not be altogether unacceptable or devoid of interest : and to the inquirer after ancient history and mythology, it may be useful to have collected into one small volume, the scattered relics for which he must otherwise search so widely.

THE

THEOLOGY OF THE PHŒNICIANS;

FROM

SANCHONIATHO.

SANCHONIATHO.

THE COSMOGONY.

ΤΗΝ των ὁλων αρχην ὑπο-
τιθεται Αερα ζοφωδη και
πνευματωδη, η πνοην αερος
ζοφαδους, και Χαος θολερον,
ερεβωδες. ταυτα δε ειναι
απειρα, και δια πολυν αιωνα
μη εχειν περας. ὁτε δε (φησιν) ηρασθη το πνευμα των
ιδιων αρχων, και εγενετο συγ-
κρασις, ἡ πλοκη εκεινη εκληθη
Ποθος αύτη δε αρχη κτισεως
ἁπαντων. αυτο δε ουκ εγινωσκε
την αυτου κτισιν, και εκ της
αυτου συμπλοκης του πνευμα-
τος, εγενετο Μωτ. τουτο τινες
φασιν ιλυν. οἱδε, ὑδατωδους
μιξεως σηψιν. και εκ ταυτης
εγενετο πασα σπορα κτισεως,
και γενεσις των ὁλων.

Ἡ δε τινα ζωα ουκ εχοντα
αισθησιν, εξ ὡν εγενετο ζωα

He supposes that the beginning of all things was a dark and condensed windy air, or a breeze of dark air and a Chaos turbid and indistinct like Erebus · and that these things were infinite, and for a long time had no bound · but when this wind became enamoured of its own principles, and a mixture took place, that embrace was called Desire : and it was the beginning of the creation of all things. But the wind knew not its own production. And of that wind from its embrace was begotten Mòt, which some call Mud, others the putrefaction of a watery mixture : and from this sprung all the seed of the creation, and the generation of the universe.

But there were certain animals which had no sense, out of which pro-

νοερα, και εκλῃθη Ζωφασημιν,
τουτ' εστιν ουρανου κατοπται.
και ανεπλασθη ὁμοιως ῳου
σχηματι, και εξελαμψε Μωτ,
Ἡλιος τε και Σεληνη, Αστερες
τε και Αστρα μεγαλα.

Και του αερος διαυγασαν-
τος, δια πυρωσιν και της θαλασσης και της γης εγενετο
πνευματα, και νεφη, και ουρα-
νιων ὑδατων μεγισται κατα-
φοραι και χυσεις και επειδη
διεκριθη, και του ιδιου τοπου
διεχωρισθη δια την του ἡλιου
πυρωσιν, και παντα συνηντησε
παλιν εν αερι ταδε τοισδε,
και συνερραξαν, βρονται τε
απετελεσθησαν και αστραπαι,
και προς τον παταγον των
βροντων τα προγεγραμμενα
νοερα ζωα εγρηγορησεν, και
προς τον ηχον επτυρη, και
εκινηθη εν τη γη και θαλασση
αρρεν και θηλυ

(Τουτοις ἑξης ὁ αυτος συγγραφευς επιφερει λεγων)
ταυθ' εὑρεθη εν τη κοσμογονια
γεγραμμενα Τααυτου, και
τοις εκεινου ὑπομνημασιν, εκ
τε στοχασμων και τεκμηριων,
ὡν ἑωρακεν αυτου ἡ διανοια,
και εὑρε, και ἡμιν εφωτισεν.

Ἑξης τουτοις ονοματα των
ανεμων ειπων Νοτου και Βο-
ρεου και των λοιπων, επιλεγει.

ceeded intelligent animals, and they were called Zophasemin, that is, the inspectors of heaven, and they were moulded in like manner in the shape of an egg, and Môt shone forth the sun and the moon, the less and the greater stars

And the air shining thoroughly with light, by its fiery influence on the sea and earth, winds were produced, and clouds, and very great defluxions, and torrents of the heavenly waters. And when these things, by the heat of the sun, were parted and separated from their proper places, and all met again in the air, and were dashed to pieces against each other, thunders and lightnings were the effect, and at the sound of the thunders, the before-mentioned intelligent animals were awakened, and frightened by the noise, and male and female moved upon the earth, and in the sea.

(After these things our Author proceeds to say.) These things are written in the Cosmogony of Taautus, and in his memoirs, and from the conjectures, and natural signs which his mind perceived and discovered, and wherewith he has enlightened us

Afterwards, declaring the names of the winds North, South, and the rest, he makes this epilogue.—But these

Αλλ' ούτοιγε πρωτοι αφιερωσαν τα της γης βλαστηματα,
και θεους ενομισαν, και προσ-
εγυνουν ταιτα, αφ' ών αυτοι
τε διεγινοντο, και οί επομενοι,
και οί προ αυτων παντες, και
χοας και επιθυσεις εποιουν.
(και επιλεγει) αύται δε ησαν
αί επινοιαι της προσκυνησεως,
όμοιαι τη αυτων ασθενεια και
ψυχης ατολμια.

first men consecrated the plants of the
earth, and judged them gods, and
worshipped those things, upon which
they themselves lived, and all their
posterity, and all before them, to
these they made libations and sacrifices. Then he proceeds :—Such were
the devices of worship, agreeing with
their weakness and the want of bold-
ness of their souls —*Euseb. Præp.*
Evan. lib. I c. 10.

THE GENERATIONS.

Ειτα (φησι) γεγεννησθαι εκ
του Κολπια ανεμου, και γυναικος αυτου Βααυ, τουτο δε
νυκτα έρμηνευειν, Αιωνα και
Πρωτογονον θνητους ανδρας,
ούτω καλουμενους, εύριν δε
τον Αιωνα την απο των δεν-
δρων τροφην.

Of the wind Colpias, and his wife
Baan, which is interpreted Night,
were begotten two mortals, called Æon
and Protogonus : and Æon found out
food from trees.

Εκ τουτων τοις γενομε-
νους ιι ηθηναι Γενος και Γενεαν, και οικησαι την Φοι-
νιγην. αυχμων δε γενομενων,
τας χειρας ορεγειν εις ουρανους
προς τον 'Ηλιον τουτον γαρ
(φησι) θεον ενομιζον μονον
ουρανου Κυριον, Βεελσαμην
καλουντες, ό εστι παρα Φοινιξι κυριος ουρανου, Ζευς δε
παρ' Ελλησι.

Those that were begotten of
these were called Genus and Genea,
and they dwelt in Phœnicia. and
when there were great droughts they
stretched forth their hands to heaven
towards the Sun ; for him they thought
the only lord of heaven, calling him
Beelsamin, which in Phœnician is
Lord of Heaven, but in the Greek
Zeus

'Εξης (φησιν) απο Γενους
Αιωνος και Πρωτογονου, γενη-

Afterwards by Genus, the son of
Protogonus and Æon, were begotten

θηναι αυθις παιδας θνητοις, οις ειναι ονοματα Φας και Πυρ και Φλοξ. ούτοι (φησιν) ε/ παρατριβης ξιλων εύρον πυρ, ναι την χρησιν εδιδαξα/

Τίοις δε εγεννησαν ούτοι μεγεθει τε και ύπεροχη /ρεισσονας. ών τα ονοματα τοις ορεσιν επιτεθη ών εκρατησαν. ώς εξ αιτων λ/ηθηναι το Κασσιον, και τον Λιβανον, και το/ Αντιλιβανον, ναι το Βραθυ.

Ε/ τουτων (φησιν) εγεννηθησαν Μημρουμος ὁ και Ύψουρανιος απο μητερων δε (φησιν,) εχρηματιζο/των τοτε γυναικων αναιδη/ μισγομενων οίς α/ εντυχοιεν. Ειτα (φησι) τον Ύψουρανιον οικησαι Τιρον, ναλυβας τε επινοησαι απο ναλαμων και θριων, και παπιρων. στασιασαι δε προς τον αδελφον Ουσωον. ός σκεπην τω σωματι πρωτος εν δερματων, ών ισχυσε συλλαβειν θηριων εύρε. 'Ραγδαιων δε γενομενων ομβρων και πνευματων, παρατριβεντα τα εν τη Τυρω δενδρα, πυρ αναψαι, και την αυτοθ. ύλην ναταφλεξαι. δενδρου δε λαβομενο/ τον Ουσωον και απον/αδεισαντα, πρωτον τολμησαι εις θαλασσαν εμβηναι· α/ιερωσαι δε δυο στηλας πυρι τε και πνευματι, και προσκινησαι, άμα τε σπενδειν

mortal children, whose names were Phós, Pûr, and Phlox. These found out the method of producing fire by rubbing pieces of wood against each other, and taught men the use thereof.

These begat sons of vast bulk and height, whose names were given to the mountains on which they first seised thus from them were named Mount Cassius, and Libanus, Antilibanus, and Brathu.

Memrumus and Hypsuranius were the issue of these men having intercourse with their mothers, the women of those times, without shame, lying with any man they chanced to meet. Then Hypsuranius inhabited Tyre: and he invented the making of huts of reeds and rushes, and the papyrus. And he fell into enmity with his brother Usous, who first made clothing for the body of the skins of the wild beasts which he could catch And when there were violent storms of rain and wind, the trees in Tyre being rubbed against each other, took fire, and the forest there was consumed. And Usous having taken a tree, and broken off its boughs, first dared to venture on the sea And he consecrated two pillars to Fire and Wind, and worshipped them, and poured out to them the blood of the wild beasts he took in hunting: and when there was an end of these (the storm and fire?)

αυταις εξ ὡν ἡγρευε θηριων. τουτων δε τελευτησαντων, τους απολειφθεντας (φησι) ῥαβδους αυτοις αφιερωσαι, και τας στηλας προσκυνειν, και τουτοις ἑορτας αγειν ϰατ'ετος.

Χρονοις δε ὑστερον πολλοις απο της Ὑψουρανιου γενεας γενεσθαι Αγρεα ϰαι Ἁλιεα, τους ἁλειας και αγρας εὑρετας. εξ ὡν κληθηναι αγρευτας και ἁλιεις.

Εξ ὡν γενεσθαι δυο αδελφους σιδηρου εὑρετας, και της τουτου εργασιας. ὡν θατερον τον χρυσωρ λογους ασϰησαι, ϰαι επᾳδας ϰαι μαντειας. ειναι δε τουτον τον Ἡφαιστον. εὑρειν δε ϰαι αγνιστρον, ϰαι δελεαρ, και ὁρμιαν, και σχεδιαν· πρωτον τε παντων ανθρωπων πλευσαι. διο και ὡς Θεον αυτον μετα θανατον εσεβασθησαν. καλεισθαι δε αυτον ϰαι Διαμιχιον. οἱ δε τους αδελφους αυτου τοιχους φασιν επινοησαι εκ πλινθων.

Μετα ταυτ' εκ του γενους τουτου γενεσθαι νεανιδας δυο, καλεισθαι δε αυτων τον μεν Τεχνιτην· τον δε Γηινον Αυτοχθονα. οὑτοι επενοησαν τῳ πηλῳ της πλινθου συμμιγνυειν φορυτον, και τῳ ἡλιῳ αυτας ϰερσαινειν. αλλα και στεγας εξευρον.

he consecrated to them the stumps of wood that remained, and worshipped the pillars, and held anniversary feasts unto the stumps.

And in the times after the generation of Hypsuranius, were Agrcus and Halieus, the inventors of the arts of hunting and fishing, from whom huntsmen and fishermen are named.

Of these were begotten two brothers who discovered iron, and the forging thereof. One of these called Chrysor, who is the same with Hephæstus, exercised himself in words, and charms, and divinations, and he invented the hook, bait, and fishing-line, and boats slightly built, and he was the first of all men that sailed. Wherefore he was worshipped after his death as a God, and called Diamichius. And it is said his brothers invented the way of making walls of bricks.

Afterwards, from this generation were born two youths, one of whom was called Technites, the other Geinus Autochthôn. These discovered the method of mingling stubble with the loam of the bricks, and of drying them in the sun; and found out tiling.

Απο τουτων εγενοντο έτεροι, ὧν ὁ μεν Αγρος εκαλειτο. ὁ δε Αγρουηρος ἡ Αγροτης. οὐ και ξοανον ειναι μαλα σεβασμιον, και ναον ζυγοφορουμενον εν Φοινικη. παρα δε Βιβλιοις εξαιρετως θεων ὁ μεγιστος ονομαζεται. επινοησαν δε οὑτοι αυλας προστιθεναι τοις οικοις, και περιβολαια, και σπηλαια εκ τουτων αγροται και κυνηγοι. οὑτοι δε και Αληται και Τιτανες καλουνται.

Απο τουτων γενεσθαι Αμυνον και Μαγον. οἱ κατεδειξαν κωμας και ποιμνας

Απο τουτων γενεσθαι Μισωρ και Συδυκ. τουτ' εστιν ευλυτον και δικαιον. οὑτοι την του ἁλος χρησιν εὑρον.

Απο Μισωρ Τααυτος. ὁς εὑρε την των πρωτων στοιχειων γραφην. εν Αιγυπτιοι μεν Θωωρ, Αλεξανδρεις δε Θωιθ, Ἑλληνες δ' Ἑρμην εκαλεσαν. εκ δε του Συδυκ, Διοσκουροι, η Καβειροι, η Κορυβαντες, η Σαμοθρακες. οὑτοι (φησι) πρωτοι πλοιον εὑρον.

Εν τουτων γεγονασιν έτεροι, οἱ και βοτανας εὑρον, και την των δακετων ιασιν, και επωδας.

Κατα τουτους γινεται τις Ηλιουν καλουμενος Ὑψιστος· και θηλεια λεγομενη Βηρουθ.

By these were begotten others, of which one was called Agrus, the other Agrouerus or Agrotes, of whom in Phœnicia there was a statue held in the highest veneration, and a temple drawn by yokes of oxen · and at Byblus he is called, by way of eminence, the greatest of the Gods These invented courts, and fences for houses, and caves or cellars: husbandmen, and such as hunt with dogs, derive their origin from these · they are called also Aletœ, and Titans.

From these were descended Amynus and Magus, who taught men to construct villages and tend flocks.

By these men were begotten Misor and Sydyc, that is, Well-freed and Just. and they found out the use of salt.

From Misor came Taautus, who invented the writing of the first letters; him the Egyptians called Thooi, the Alexandrians Thoyth, and the Greeks Hermes. But from Sydyc came the Dioscuri, or Cabiri, or Corybantes, or Samothraces · these (he says) first built a ship complete

From these descended others, who discovered medicinal herbs, and the cure of poisons and charms.

Contemporary with these was one Elioun, which imports Hypsistus, (the most high) and his wife called

οἱ καὶ κατώκουν περὶ Βυβλον.
ἐξ ὦν γεναται Επιγειος η
Αυτοχθων ὁν ὑστερον εκαλεσαν Ουρανον. ὡς απ' αυτου
και το ὑπερ ἡμας στοιχειον,
δι' ὑπερβολην του καλλευς ονο-
μαζειν Ουρανον· γεναται δε
τουτῳ αδελφη εκ των προειρη-
μενων. ἡ δε εκληθη Γη και δια
το καλλος, απ' αυτη; (φησιν)
εκαλεσαν την ὁμωνυμον Γην.

Ὁ δε τουτων πατηρ ὁ
Ὑψιςος εκ συμβολης θηριων τε-
λευθησας αφιερωθη ᾡ και χοας
και θυσιας οἱ παιδες ετελεσαν.

Παραλαβων δε ὁ Ουρανος
την του πατρος αρχην, αγεται
προς γαμον την αδελφην Γην,
και ποιειται εξ αυτης παιδας
δ'. Ιλον, τον και Κρονον, και
Βετυλον, και Δαγων, ὁς εστι
σιτων, και Ατλαντα

Και εξ αλλων δε γαμετων
ὁ Ουρανος πολλην εσχε γενεαν.
διο και χαλεπαινουσα ἡ Γη,
τον Ουρανον ζηλοτυπουσα
εκακιζεν, ὡς και διαστηναι
αλληλων. ὁ δε Ουρανος απο-
χωρησας αυτης μετα βιας,
ὁτε και εβουλετο επιων και
πλησιαζων αυτη, παλιν απ-
ηλλατετο. επεχειρει δε και
τους εξ αυτης παιδας διαφ-
θειρειν την δε Γην αμυνασθαι
πολλακις, συμμαχιαν αυτη
συλλεξαμενην

Beruth, and they dwelt about Byblus; of whom was begotten Epigeus
or Autochthon, whom they afterwards
called Ouranus (Heaven); so that
from him that element, which is over
us, by reason of its excellent beauty
is named heaven: and he had a sister
of the same parents, and she was
called Ge (Earth), and by reason of
her beauty the earth was called by the
same name.

Hypsistus, the father of these,
having been killed in a conflict with
wild beasts, was consecrated, and his
children offered libations and sacrifices
unto him.

But Ouranus, taking the kingdom
of his father, married his sister Ge,
and had by her four sons, Ilus who
is called Cronus, and Betylus, and
Dagon who is Siton, and Atlas.

But by other wives Ouranus had
much issue; whereat Ge, being grieved
and jealous, reproached Ouranus, so
that they parted from each other·
but Ouranus, though he had parted
from her, yet by force returned when-
ever he pleased, and having laid with
her again departed, moreover he
attempted to kill the children he had
by her, Ge also often defended or
avenged herself, gathering unto her
auxiliary powers

c

Εις ανδρα· δε προελθων ὁ
Κρονος, Ἑρμῃ τω τρισμε-
γιστω συμβουλῳ και βοηθῳ
χρωμενος, ουτος γαρ ην αυτου
γραμματευς, τον πατερα Ουρανον αμυνεται, τιμωρων τῃ
μητρι. Κρονου δε γινονται
παιδες, Περσεφονη και Αθηνα
ἡ μεν ουν πρωτη, παρθενος
ετελευτα. της δε Αθηνας γνω-
μῃ και Ἑρμου κατεσκευασε
Κρονος εκ σιδηρου ἁρπην και
δορυ Ειτα ὁ Ἑρμης τοις του
Κρονου συμμαχοις λογους μα-
γειας διαλεχθεις, ποθον ενε-
ποιησε τοις κατ' Ουρανον μα-
χης ὑπερ της Γης και οὑτω
Κρονος τον Οιρανον πολεμω
συμβαλων, της αρχης ηλασε,
και την βασιλειαν διεδεξατο
Ἑαλω δε εν τῃ μαχῃ και ἡ
επεραστος του Ουρανου συγ-
κοιτος εγκυμων ουσα ἡν εκδι-
δωσιν ὁ Κρονος προς γαμον τῳ
Δαγωνι τικτει δε παρα τουτῳ
ὁ κατα γαστρος εξ Ουρανου
εφερεν ὁ δε εκαλεσε Δημαρουν

Επι τουτοις ὁ Κρονος τειχος
περιβαλλει τῃ ἑαυτου οικησει,
και πρωτην πολιν κτιζει την επ.
Φοινικης Βυβλον. Μετα ταυτα
τον αδελφον τον ιδιον Ατλαντα
ὑπονοησας ὁ Κρονος, μετα
γνωμης τ Ἑρμου εις βαθος
γης εμβαλων κατεχωσε.

Κατα τουτον τον χρονον οἱ

But when Cronus came to man's
age, by the advice and assistance of
Hermes Trismegistus, who was his
secretary, he opposed his father
Ouranus, that he might avenge his
mother. And Cronus had children,
Persephone and Athena, the former
died a virgin; but, by the advice of
Athena and Hermes, Cronus made of
iron a scimitar and a spear. Then
Hermes, addressing the allies of Cronus with magic words, wrought in
them a keen desire to fight against
Ouranus in behalf of Ge. And thus
Cronus overcoming Ouranus in battle,
drove him from his kingdom, and
succeeded him in the imperial power
In the battle was taken a well-beloved
concubine of Ouranus who was preg-
nant, Cronus gave her in marriage
to Dagon, and she was delivered, and
called the child Demaroon.

After these events Cronus builds a
wall round about his habitation, and
founds Byblus, the first city of
Phœnicia Afterwards Cronus sus-
pecting his own brother Atlas, by the
advice of Hermes, threw him into a
deep cavern in the earth, and buried
him

At this time the descendants of the

απο των Διοσκουρων σχεδιας και πλοια συνθεντες, επλευσαν. και ενριφεντες κατα το Κασσιον ορος, ναον αυτοθι αφιερωσαν.

Οἱ δε συμμαχοι Ιλου του Κρονου Ελωειμ επεκληθησαν, ὡς αν Κρονιοι οὑτοι ησαν οἱ λεγομενοι επι Κρονου Κρονος δε ὑον εχων Σαδιδον, δι αυτον σιδηρω διεχρησατο, δι᾽ ὑπονοιας αυτον εσχηκως και της ψυχης, αυτοχειρ του παιδος γενομενος, εστερησεν ὡσαυτως και θυγατρος .δίας την κεφαλην απετεμεν ὡς παντας εκπεπληχθαι θεους την Κρονου γνωμην.

Χρονου δε προιοντος Ουρανος εν φυγη τυγχανων, θυγατερα αυτου παρθενον Ασταρτην μεθ᾽ ετερων αυτης αδελφων δυο, Ρέας και Διωνης δολω τον Κρονον ανελειν ὑποπεμπει· ἁς και ἑλων ὁ Κρονος κουριδιας γαμετας αδελφας ουσας εποιησατο. Γνους δε ὁ Ουρανος, επιστρατευει κατα του Κρονου Εἱμαρμενην και Ὡραν μεθ᾽ ετεραν συμμαχαν και ταυτας εξοικειωσαμενος ὁ Κρονος, παρ᾽ ἑαυτω κατεσχεν. ετι δε (φησιν) επενοησε θεος Ουρανος Βαιτυλια, λιθους εμψυχους μηχανησαμενος

Κρονω δε εγενοντο απο

Dioscuri, having built some light and other more complete ships, put to sea; and being out over against Mount Cassius, there consecrated a temple.

But the auxiliaries of Ilus, who is Cronus, were called Eloim, (as it were) the allies of Cronus; they were so called after Cronus And Cronus, having a son called Sadidus, dispatched him with his own sword, because he held him in suspicion, and with his own hand deprived his son of life. And in like manner he cut off the head of his own daughter, so that all the gods were amazed at the mind of Cronus

But in process of time, Ouranus being in banishment, sent his daughter Astarte, with two other sisters, Rhea and Dione, to cut off Cronus by deceit; but Cronus took the damsels, and married them being his own sisters. Ouranus, understanding this, sent Eimarmene and Hora with other auxiliaries to make war against him. but Cronus gained the affections of these also, and kept them with himself Moreover, the god Ouranus devised Bætulia, contriving stones that moved as having life.

And Cronus begat on Astarte seven

Ασταρτης θυγατερε; ἑπτα Τιτανιδες η Αρτεμιδες. και παλιν τῳ αυτῳ γινονται απο Ρέας παιδες ἑπτα, ὡν ὁ νεωτατος ἁμα τη γενεσει ἀφιέρωθη, και απο Διωνης θηλεια και απο Ασαρτης παλιν αῤῥενες δυο, Ποθος και Ερως

daughteis called Titanides, or Artemides, and he begat on Rhea seven sons, the youngest of whom was consecrated from his birth; also by Dione he had daughteis, and by Astarte moreovei two sons, Pothos and Eros

'Ο δε Δαγων επειδη εἱρε σιτον και αροτρον, εκληθη Ζευς Αροτριος

And Dagon, after he had found out bread-coin and the plough, was called Zeus Arotrius.

Συδυκῳ δε τῳ λεγομενῳ δικαιῳ, μια των Τιτανιδων συνελθουσα, γεννα τον Ασκληπιον εγενηθησαν δε και εν Περαιᾳ Κρονῳ, τρεις παιδες, Κρονος ὁμωνυμος τῳ πατρι, και Ζευς Βηλος, και Απολλων

To Sydyc, called the just, one of the Titanides bare Asclepius · Cronus had also in Peræa three sons, Cronus beaiing his father's name, and Zeus Belus, and Apollo

Κατα τουτους γινονται Ποντος και Τυφων και Νηρευς, πατηρ Ποντου. απο δε του Ποντου γινεται Σιδων· ἡ καθ' ὑπερβολην ευφωνιας πρωτη ὑμνον ᾠδης εὑρε. και Ποσειδων

Contemporary with these were Pontus, and Typhon, and Nereus the father of Pontus. from Pontus descended Sidon, who by the excellence of her singing first invented the hymns of odes or piaises · and Posidon

Τῳ δε Δημαρουντι γινεται Μελικαρθος. ὁ και Ἡρακλης.

But to Demaroon was born Melicarthus, who is also called Heracles

Ειτα παλιν Ουρανος πολεμει Ποντῳ και αποστας, Δημαρουντι προστιθεται. Επεισι τε Ποντω ὁ Δημαρους, τροποιται τε αυτον ὁ Ποντος ὁ δε Δημαρους φυγης θυσιαν ηυξατο

Then again Ouranus makes war against Pontus, but paiting from him attaches himself to Demaroon Demaroon invades Pontus, but Pontus puts him to flight, and Demaroon vows a sacrifice for his escape.

Ετει δε τριακοστῳ δευτερῳ της ἑαυτου κρατησεως και βασιλειας, ὁ Ιλος, τουτ' εστιν

In the thirty-second yeai of his power and reign, Ilus, who is Cionus, having laid an ambuscade for his

ὁ Κρονος, Ουρανον τον πατερα
λοχησας εν τοπῳ τινι μεσο-
γειῳ, και λαβων ὑποχειριον,
εντεμνει αυτου τα αιδοια, συν-
εγγυς πηγων τε και ποταμων.
ενθα ἀφιερωθη Ουρανος, και
απηρτισθη αυτου το πνευμα,
και απεσταξεν αυτου το αἱμα
των αιδοιων, εις τας πηγας,
και των ποταμων τα ὑδατα,
και μεχρι τουτου δεικνυται το
χωριον

(Παλιν δε ὁ συγγραφευς
τουτοις επιφερει μεθ' ἑτερα
λεγων.) Ασταρτη δε ἡ μεγιστη,
και Ζευς Δημαρους,
και Αδωδος βασιλευς θεων,
εβασιλευον της χωρας, Κρονου
γνωμη ἡ δε Ασταρτη επεθηκε
τῃ ιδιᾳ κεφαλῃ βασιλειας
παρασημον κεφαλην ταυρου.
περινοστουσα δε την οικουμενην, εὑρεν αεροπετη αστερα,
ὁν και ανελομενη, εν Τυρῳ τῃ
ἁγιᾳ νησῳ αφιερασε (Την δε
Ασταρτην Φοινικες, την Ἀφρο-
διτην ειναι λεγουσι.)

Και ὁ Κρονος δε περιων
την οικουμενην, Αθηνᾳ τῃ ἑαυτου θυγατρι διδωσι της Αττικης
την βασιλειαν λοιμου δε γε-
νομενου και φθορας, τον ἑαυτου
μονογενη υἱον, Κρονος Ουρανῳ
πατρι ὁλοκαρποι, και τα αιδοια
περιτεμνεται, ταυτο ποιησαι
και τους ἀφ' αυτῳ συμμαχους

father Ouranus in a certain place in
the middle of the earth, and having
gotten him into his hands, dismem-
bers him near fountains and rivers
There Ouranus was consecrated, and
his spirit was separated, and the
blood of his parts dropt into the fountains and the waters of the rivers; and
the place is shewed even to this day

(Then our historian, after some
other things, goes on thus.) But
Astarte called the greatest, and Demaroon entitled Zeus, and Adodus
named the king of gods, reigned over
the country by the consent of Cronus
and Astarte put upon her head, as
the mark of her sovereignty, a bull's
head: and travelling about the habi-
table world, she found a star falling
through the air, which she took up,
and consecrated in the holy island
Tyre. and the Phœnicians say that
Astarte is Aphrodite.

Cronus, also going about the habi-
table world, gave to his daughter
Athena the kingdom of Attica and
when there happened a plague and
mortality, Cronus offered up his only
son as a sacrifice to his father Ouranus, and circumcised himself, and
forced his allies to do the same: and
not long afterwards he consecrated

καταναγ/ασας και μετ' ου
πολυ έτερον αυτου παιδα απο
Ρέας ονομαζομενον Μο*θ' απο-
θανοντα αφιεροι. Θανατον
δε τουτον /αι Πλουτανα Φοινικες ονομαζουσι.

Και επι τουτοις ό Κρονος
Βιβλον μεν την πολιν θεω
Βααλτιδ., τη και Διωνη δ δω-
σι, Βηρυτον δε Ποσειδωνι /αι
Ιαβηροι: αγροταις τε /αι άλι-
ευσιν. οι και Ποντου λειψανα,
εις την Βηρυτον αφιερωσαν.

Προ δε τουτων θεος Τααυ-
τος μιμησαμενος τον Ουρανον,
των θεων οψεις, Κρονου τε και
Δαγωνος, /αι των λοιπων διε-
τυπωσεν τους ίερους των στοιχειων χαρακτηρας επενοησε
δε και τω Κρονω παρασημα
βασιλειας, ομματα τεσσαρα
ε/ των εμπροσθιων /αι των
οπισθιων μερων· δυο δε ήσυχη
μυοντα· και επι των ωμων
πτερα τεσσαρα· δυο μεν, ώς
ίπταμενα, δυο δε ώς ύφειμενα.
το δε συμβολον ην, επειδη
Κρονος κοιμαμενος εβλεπε, και
εγρηγορας εκοιματο· και επι
των πτερων όμοιως ότι ανα-
παυομενος ίπτατο, και ίπτα-
μενος ανεπαυετο· τοις δε λοι-
ποις θεοις, δυο έκαστω πτερω-
ματα επι των ωμων, ώς ότι δη
συνιπταντο τω Κρονω. και
αι'τω δε παλιν επι της κεφαλη,,,

after his death another son, called
Muth, whom he had by Rhea, him
the Phœnicians call Death and Pluto.

After these things, Cronus gives
the city of Byblus to the goddess
Baaltis, which is Dione, and Berytus
to Posidon, and to the Cabeii, the
husbandmen and fishermen and they
consecrated the remains of Pontus at
Berytus.

But before these things the god
Taautus, having represented Ouranus,
made types of the countenances of
the gods Cronus, and Dagon, and
the sacred characters of the other
elements He contrived also for Cronus the ensign of his royal power,
having four eyes in the parts before
and in the parts behind, two of them
closing as in sleep, and upon the
shoulders four wings, two in the act
of flying, and two reposing as at rest
And the symbol was, that Cronus
whilst he slept was watching, and
reposed whilst he was awake And
in like manner with respect to his
wings, that whilst he rested he was
flying, yet rested whilst he flew But
to the other gods there were two
wings only to each upon his shoulders, to intimate that they flew under
the controul of Cronus; he had also
two wings upon his head, the one for

πτερα δυο. ἐν επι του ἡγεμο-
νικωτατου νου, και ἐν επι της
αισθησεως

Ελθων δε ὁ Κρονος εις νοτου
χωραν, ἁπασαν την Αιγυπτον
εδωκε Θεῳ Τααυτῳ, ὁπως
βασιλειον αυτῳ γενηται.

Ταυτα δε (φησι) πρωτοι
αυτων ὑπεμνηματισαντο οἱ
ἑπτα Συδεκ παιδες Καβηροι,
και ογδοος αυτων αδελφος Ασκληπιος, ὡς αυτοις ενετειλατο
Θεος Τααντος.

Ταιτα παντα ὁ Θαβιωνος
παις, πρωτος των απ' αιωνος
γεγονοτων Φοινικων Ἱεροφαντης
αλληγορησας, τοις τε φυσικοις
και κοσμικοις παθεσιν αναμιξ-
ας, παρεδωκε τοις οργιωσι, και
τελετων καταρχουσι προφη-
ταις. οἱ τον τυφον αυξειν εκ
παντος επινοουντες, τοις αυτων
διαδοχοις παρεδωσαν και τοις
επεισακτοις. ὧν εἰς ην και
Ισιρις των τριων γραμματων
εὑρετης, αδελφος Χνα του πρωτου μετονομασθεντος Φοινικος.

the most governing part, the mind, and one for the sense.

And Cronus coming into the country of the south, gave all Egypt to the god Taautus, that it might be his kingdom.

These things, says he, the Caberi, the seven sons of Sydec, and their eighth brother Asclepius, first of all set down in memoirs, as the god Taautus commanded them

All these things the son of Thabion, the first Hierophant of all among the Phœnicians, allegorized and mixed up with the occurrences and passions of nature and the world, and delivered to the priests and prophets, the superintendants of the mysteries : and they, perceiving the rage for these allegories increase, delivered them to their successors, and to foreigners : of whom one was Isiris, the inventor of the three letters, the brother of Chna, who is called the first Phœnician.—
Euseb. Præp. Evan. lib. I. c. 10.

OF THE MYSTICAL SACRIFICE OF THE ~~EGYPTIANS~~ *Phœnicia's*

Εθος ην τοις παλαιοις, εν
ταις μεγαλαις συμφοραις των
κινδυνων, αντι της παντων
φθορας, το ηγατημενον των
τεκνων, τους κρατουντας η

It was the custom among the ancients, in times of great calamity, to prevent the ruin of all, for the rulers of the city or nation to sacrifice to the avenging deities the most beloved

πολεως η εθνους, εις σφαγην
επιδιδοναι λυτρον τοις τιμωροις
δαιμοσι κατεσφαττοντο δε οι
ε δομενοι μυστικως   Κρονος
τοινυν, ον οι Φοινικες Ισραηλ
(Ιλ?) προσαγορευουσι, βασι-
λευων της χωρας, και υστερον
μετα την του βιου τελευτην
εις τον του Κρονου αστερα καθ-
ιερωθεις, εξ επιχωριας νυμφης
Ανωβρετ λεγομενης, υιον εχων
μονογενη, ον δια τουτο Ιεουδ
εκαλουν, του μονογενους ουτως
ετι και νυν καλουμενου παρα
τοις Φοινιξι, κινδυνων εκ πολεμου
μεγιστων κατειληφοτων την
χωραν, βασιλικω κοσμησας
σχηματι τον υιον, βωμον τε
κατασκευασαμενος κατεθυσεν.

of their children as the price of redemption . they who were devoted for
this purpose were offered mystically.
For Cronus, whom the Phœnicians
call Il, and who after his death was
deified and instated in the planet
which bears his name, when king,
had by a nymph of the country called
Anobret an only son, who on that
account is styled Ieoud, for so the
Phœnicians still call an only son
and when great danger from war
beset the land he adorned the altar,
and invested this son with the emblems of royalty, and sacrificed him.
—*Euseb Præp. Evan.* lib I c 10

OF THE SERPENT.

Την μεν ουν του δρακοντος
φυσιν και των οφεων αυτος
εξεθειασεν ο Τααυτος, και μετ'
αυτον αυθις Φοινικες τε και
Αιγυπτιοι. πνευματικωτατον
γαρ το ζωον παντων των ερ-
πετων, και πυρωδες υπ' αυτου
παρεδοθη παρ' ω και ταχος
ανυπερβλητον δια του πνευ-
ματος παριστησι, χωρις ποδων
τε και χειρων, η αλλου τινος
των εξωθεν, εξ ων τα λοιπα
ζωα τας κινησεις ποιειται. και

Taautus first consecrated the basilisk,
and introduced the worship of the
serpent tribe; in which he was followed by the Phœnicians and Egyptians. For this animal was held by
him to be the most inspirited of all the
reptiles, and of a fiery nature; inasmuch
as it exhibits an incredible celerity, moving by its spirit without either hands,
or feet, or any of those external organs,
by which other animals effect their
motion. And in its progress it as-
sumes a variety of forms, moving in a

ποικιλων σχηματων τιπους
αποτελει, και κατα την πο-
ρειαν ἑλικοειδεις εχει τας ὁρμας,
εφ' ἱ βουλεται ταχος και
πολυχρονιωτατον δε εσϊι, ου
μονον τῳ εκδυομεϊον το γηρας
νεαζειν, αλλα και αυξησιϊ
επιδεχεσθαι μειζονα πεφυκε.
ϊαι επειδαν το ὡρισμενον με-
τρον πληρωσῃ, εις ἑαυτον αϊα-
λισκεται ὡς εν ταις ἱεραις
ὁμοιως αυτος ὁ Τααυτος ϊατε-
ταξε γραφαις. διο ϊαι εν ἱεροις
τουτο το ζωον και εν μυστη-
ριοις συμπαρειληπται.

spiral course, and at what degree of swiftness it pleases. And it is very long-lived, and has the quality not only of putting off its old age, and assuming a second youth, but it receives a greater increase. And when it has fulfilled the appointed measure of its existence, it consumes itself: as Taautus has laid down in the sacred books, wherefore this animal is introduced in the sacred rites and mysteries.—*Euseb Præp. Evan.* lib. I. c. 10.

THE FRAGMENTS

OF

THE CHALDÆAN HISTORY:

FROM

BEROSSUS, ABYDENUS, AND
MEGASTHENES.

BEROSSUS:

FROM APOLLODORUS.

OF THE CHALDÆAN KINGS.

ΤΑΥΤΑ μεν ὁ Βηρωσσος ἱστορησε. Πρωτον γενεσθαι βασιλεα Αλωρον εκ Βαβυλωνος Χαλδαιον. βασιλευται δε σαρους δεκα. και ῥαθεξης Αλαπαρον και Αμηλωνα τον εκ Παντιβιβλων. ειτα Αμμενωνα τον Χαλδαιον, εφ᾽ οὑ (φησι) φανηναι τον μυσαρον Ωαννην τον Αννηδωτον εκ της Ερυθρας (ὁπερ Αλεξανδρος προλαβων ειρηκε φανηναι τῳ πρωτῳ ετει. οὑτος δε μετα σαρους τεσσαρακοντα. ὁ δε Αβυδινος τον δευτερον Αννηδωτον μετα σαρους ει῾οσι ἑξ.) ειτα Μεγαλαρον εκ Παντιβιβλων πολεως. βασιλευται δε αυτον σαρους οκτωκαιδεκα. και μετα τουτον Δαωνον ποιμενα εκ Παντιβιβλων βασιλευται σαρους δεκα. κατα τουτον παλιν (φησι) φανηναι ε῾ της Ερυθρας Αννηδατον τεταρτον την αυτην τοις ανω

THIS is the history which Berossus has transmitted to us. He tells us that the first king was Aloius of Babylon, a Chaldæan , he reigned ten sari: and afterwards Alaparus, and Amelon who came from Pantibiblon then Ammenon the Chaldæan, in whose time appeared the Musarus Oannes the Annedotus from the Erythræan sea. (But Alexander Polyhistor anticipating the event, has said that he appeared in the first year; but Apollodorus says that it was after forty sari; Abydenus, however, makes the second Annedotus appear after twenty-six sari.) Then succeeded Megalarus from the city of Pantibiblon; and he reigned eighteen sari: and after him Daonus the shepherd from Pantibiblon reigned ten sari; in his time (he says) appeared again from the Erythræan sea a fourth Annedotus, having the same form with those above, the shape of

εχοντα διαθεσιν, και την
ιχθυος προς ανθρωπους μιξιν.
ειτα ηρξαι Ευεδωρεσχον εκ
Παντιβιβλων, και βασιλευσαι
σαρους οκτωναιδεκα. επι τουτου (φησιν) αλλον φανηναι εκ
της Ερυθρας Θαλασσης ὁμοιον
κατα την ιχθυος προς ανθρωπον μιξιν, ᾧ ονομα Οδαλων
(Τουτους δε φησι παντας τα
ὑπο Ωαννου κεφαλαιωδως ρηθεντα κατα μερος εξηγησασθαι. περι τουτων Αβυδινος
ουδεν ειπεν) ειτα αρξαι Αμεμψινον Χαλδαιον εκ Λαραγχων.
βασιλευσαι δε αυτον ογδοον
σαρους δεκα. ειτα αρξαι Ωτιαρτην Χαλδαιον εκ Λαραγχων
βασιλευσαι δε σαρους η'. Ωτιαρτου δε τελευτησαντος τον
υίον αυτου Ξισουθρον βασιλευσαι σαρους οκτωκαιδεκα. επι
τουτου τον μεγαν κατακλυσμον (φησι) γεγενησθαι. ὡς
γινεσθαι ὁμου παντας βασιλεις δεκα· σαρους δε ἑκατον
εικοσι.

a fish blended with that of a man.
Then reigned Euedoreschus from
Pantibiblon, for the term of eighteen
sari; in his days there appeared
another personage from the Erythræan sea like the former, having
the same complicated form between
a fish and a man, whose name was
Odacon. (All these, says Apollodorus, related particularly and circumstantially whatever Oannes had informed them of. concerning these
Abydenus has made no mention.)
Then reigned Amempsinus, a Chaldæan from Laranchœ; and he being
the eighth in order reigned ten sari.
Then reigned Otiartes, a Chaldæan,
from Laranchœ; and he reigned
eight sari. And upon the death of
Otiartes, his son Xisuthrus reigned
eighteen sari in his time happened
the great deluge. So that the sum
of all the kings is ten; and the term
which they collectively reigned an
hundred and twenty sari.—*Syncel.
Chron.* 39. *Euseb. Chron.* 5.

BEROSSUS:

FROM ABYDENUS.

ΧΑΛΔΑΙΩΝ μεν της σοφιης περι τοσαυτα.

Βασιλευσαι δε της χωρας πρωτον λεγει Αλωρον. τον δε ὑπερ ἑωυτου λογον διαδουναι, ὁτι μιν του λεω ποιμενα ὁ Θεος αποδειξαι. βασιλευσαι δε σαρους δελα σαρος δε εστι ἑξακοσια και τρισχιλια ετεα· νηρος δε ἑξακοσια· σωσσος δε εξηκοντα.

Μετα δε τουτον Αλαπαρον αρξαι σαρους τρεις, μεθ' ὁν Αμιλλαρος εκ πολεως Παντιβιβλιος εβασιλευσεν σαρους ιγ'. εφ' οὑ δευτερον Αννηδωτον την θαλασσαν αναδυναι παραπλησιον Ωαννη την ιδεαν ἡμιδαιμονα. μεθ' ὁν Αμμενων εκ Παντιβιβλων ηρξε σαρους ιβ'. μεθ' ὁν Μεγαλαρος εκ Παντιβιβλων ηρξε σαρους οκτωκαιδεκα. ειτα Δαως ποιμην εκ Παντιβιβλων εβασιλευσεν

So much concerning the wisdom of the Chaldæans.

It is said that the first king of the country was Alorus, who gave out a report that he was appointed by God to be the Shepherd of the people: he reigned ten sari now a sarus is esteemed to be three thousand six hundred years, a neros six hundred, and a sossus sixty.

After him Alaparus reigned three sari · to him succeeded Amillarus from the city of Pantibiblon, who reigned thirteen sari; in his time a semidæmon called Annedotus, very like to Oannes, came up a second time from the sea · after him Ammenon reigned twelve sari, who was of the city of Pantibiblon : then Megalarus of the same place eighteen sari · then Daos, the shepherd, governed for the space of ten sari; he was of Pantibiblon; in his time

σαρους δεκα, εφ' ου δ' διφυεις
γην εκ θαλασσης ανεδισαν,
ωντα ονομαla ταυla· Ευεδω-
λος, Ενενγαμος, Ενευβολος,
Ανημεντος. επι δε του μετα
ταυτα Ευεδαρεσχοι Ανωδαφος·
μεθ' ους αλλοιτε ηρξαν, και
Σεισιθρος επι τοιτοις. ως τους
παντας ειναι βασιλεις δενα·
ών ὁ χρονος της βασιλειας συν-
ηρξε σαρους ἑκατον εικοσι.
(και περι του κατακλυσμου,
παρ' ὁμοια μεν ουκ απαραλ-
λακτα λεγει ουτως) μετ'
Ευεδωρεσχον αλλοι τινες ηρξαν
και Σεισιθρος· ᾧ δη Κρονος
προσημαινει μεν εσεσθαι πληθος ομβρων Δεσιου πεμπτη επι
δενα. κελευει δε παν ὁ,τι γραμματων ην εχομενον, εν ἡλιου
πολει τη εν Σιππαροισιν απο
κρυψαι. Σεισιθρος δε ταυτα
επιτελεα ποιησας, ευθεως επ'
Αρμενιους ανεπl ωε, και παραυ-
τικα μιν κατελαμβανε τα εν
θεοι Τριτη δε ἡμερη επειτα
ών εκοπασε, μετηει των ορνιθων
πειργν ποιευμενος, εικου γην
ιδοιεν του ὑδατος ελδυσαν. Αἱ
δε ελδεχομενου σφεας πελαγεος
αχανεος, απορεουσαι ὁκη καθορ-
μησονται, παρα τον Σεισιθρον
οπισω κομιζονται, και επ' αυ-
τησιν ετεραι 'Ως δε τησι
τριτησι ευτυχεεν, απικατο γαρ
δη πηλου καταπλεοι τους ταρ-

four double-shaped personages came
out of the sea to land, whose names
were Euedocus, Eneugamus, Eneu-
boulus, and Anementus : after these
things was Anodaphus, in the time of
Euedoreschus. There were afterwards
other kings, and last of all Sisithrus :
so that in the whole, the number
amounted to ten kings, and the term
of their reigns to an hundred and
twenty sari (And among other things
not irrelative to the subject, he con-
tinues thus concerning the deluge .)
After Euedoreschus some others
reigned, and then Sisithrus. To him
the deity Cronus foretold that on the
fifteenth day of the month Desius
there would be a deluge, and commanded him to deposit all the writings
whatever that he had, in the city of
the Sun in Sippara. Sisithrus, when
he had complied with these commands, instantly sailed to Armenia,
and was immediately inspired by
God. During the prevalence of the
waters Sisithrus sent out birds, that
he might judge if the flood had sub-
sided. But the birds passing over
an unbounded sea, and not finding
any place of rest, returned again to
Sisithrus This he repeated. And
when upon the third trial he succeeded, for they then returned with
their feet stained with mud, the gods
translated him from among men.
With respect to the vessel, which yet

σους, Θεοι μιν εξ ανθρωπων
αφανιζουσιν. Το δε πλοιον εν
Αρμενιη περιαπτα ξυλων αλεξι-
φαρμακα τοισιν επιχωριοισι
παρειχετο.

remains in Armenia, it is a custom
of the inhabitants to form bracelets
and amulets of its wood.—*Syncel.*
38. — *Euseb Præp. Evan* lib. 9. —
Euseb Chron. 5. 8

OF THE TOWER OF BABEL.

Εντι δ' οἱ λεγουσι τους
πρωτους εκ γης ανασχοντας,
ρωμη τε και μεγεθει χαυνω-
θεντας, και δη Θεων κατα-
φρονησαντας, ἱαμεινονας ειναι,
πυργων τυρσιν ἡλιβατον αειρειν,
ἱνα νυν Βαβυλων εστιν· ηδη τε
ασσον ειναι του ουρανου. και
τους ανεμοις, θεοισι βωθεοντας
ανατρεψαι περι αυτοισι το
μηχανημα. του δητα ερειπια
λεγεσθαι Βαβυλωνα. τεως δε
οντας ὁμογλωσσους εκ Θεων
πολυθρα φωνην ενειναοθαι,
μετα δε Κρονω τε και Τιτηνι
συστηναι πολεμον. ὁ δε τοπος
εν ᾧ πυργον ᾠκοδομησαν, νυν
Βαβυλων καλειται, δια την
συγχυσιν του περι την διαλεκτον πρωτον εναγρους. 'Εβραιοι
γαρ την συγχυσιν Βαβελ
καλουσι

They say that the first inhabitants
of the earth, glorying in their own
strength and size, and despising the
gods, undertook to raise a tower whose
top should reach the sky, where
Babylon now stands : but when it
approached the heaven, the winds
assisted the gods, and overturned
the work upon its contrivers : and
its ruins are said to be at Babylon ·
and the gods introduced a diversity
of tongues among men, who till
that time had all spoken the same
language :   and a war arose between Cronus and Titan · but the
place in which they built the tower
is now called Babylon, on account of
the confusion of the tongues; for confusion is by the Hebrews called Babel
—*Euseb. Præp Evan.* lib. 9.—*Syncel.
Chron.* 44 —*Euseb. Chron.* 13.

BEROSSUS:

FROM ALEXANDER POLYHISTOR.

OF THE COSMOGONY ~~AND CAUSES OF~~ *Cannes and* THE DELUGE.

ΒΗΡΩΣΣΟΣ δε εν τη πρατη των Βαβυλωνιακων φησι, γενεσθαι μεν αυτον κατα Αλεξανδρον τον Φιλιππου την ἡλικιαν. αναγραφας δε πολλων εν Βαβυλωνι φυλασσεσθαι μετα πολλης επιμελειας απο ετων που ὑπερ μυριαδων δεκακαιπεντε περιεχουσας χρονον περιεχειν δε τας αναγραφας ἱστοριας περι του ουρανου, και θαλασσης, και πρωτογονιας, και βασιλεων, και των κατ' αυτους πραξεων.

Και πρωτον μεν την Βαβυλωνιαν γην (φησι) νεισθαι ετι του Τιγριδος και Ευφρατου ποταμου μεσην. φυειν δε αυτην πυρους αγριους, και κριθας, και οχρον, και σησαμον, και τας εν τοις ἑλεσι φυομενας ῥιζας εσθιεσθον ονομαζεσθαι αυτας γογγας· ισοδυναμειν δε τας ῥιζας

BEROSSUS, in his first book concerning the history of Babylonia, informs us that he lived in the time of Alexander the son of Philip And he mentions that there were written accounts preserved at Babylon with the greatest care, comprehending a term of fifteen myriads of years. These writings contained a history of the heavens and the sea, of the birth of mankind; also of those who had sovereign rule; and of the actions achieved by them.

And in the first place he describes Babylonia as a country which lay between the Tigris and Euphrates He mentions that it abounded with wheat, barley, ocrus, sesamum; and in the lakes were found the roots called gongæ, which were good to be eaten, and were in respect to nutriment like barley There were also palm trees and apples, and most

ταυτας κριθαις. γινεσθαι δε
φοινικας, και μηλα, και τα
λοιπα αγροδρυα, και ιχθυας
και ορνεα, χερσαια τε και
λιμναια. ειναι δε αυτης τα μεν
κατα Αραβ αν μερη ανδρα τε
και ακαρπα, τα δε αντικει-
μενα τη Αραβια, ορεινα τε και
ευφορα εν δε τη Βαβυλωνι
πολυ πληθος ανθρωπων γενεσθαι
αλλοεθνων κατοικησαντων την
Χαλδαιαν· ζην δε αυτους αλακ-
τως, ὡσπερ τα θηρια.

Εν δε τῳ πρωτῳ ενιαυτῳ φανηναι εκ της Ερυθρας θαλασσης
κατα τον ὁμορρουντα τοπον τη
Βαβυλωνια ζωον αφρενον ονοματι
Ωαννην, (καθως και Απολλο-
δωρος ἱστορησε,) το μεν ὁλον
σωμα εχον ιχθυος· ὑπο δε την
κεφαλην παραπεφυκυιαν αλλην
κεφαλην ὑπο κατω της του
ιχθυος κεφαλης, και ποδας
ὁμοιως ανθρωπου, παραπεφυ-
κοτας δε εκ της ουρας του
ιχθυος ειναι δε αυτῳ φωνην
ανθρωπου, την δε εικονα αυτου
ετι και νυν διαφυλασσεσθαι.

Τουτο δε (φησιν) το ζωον
την μεν ἡμεραν διατριβειν μετα
των ανθρωπων, μηδεμιαν τροφην
προσφερομενον· παραδιδοναι τε
τοις ανθρωποις γραμματων,
και μαθηματων, και τεχνων
παντοδαπων εμπειριαν, και
πολεων συνοικισμους, και ἱερων

kinds of fruits, fish too and birds; both those which are merely of flight, and those which take to the element of water. The part of Babylonia which is bordered upon Arabia, was barren, and without water; but that which lay on the other side had hills, and was fruitful. At Babylon there was (in these times) a great resort of people of various nations, who inhabited Chaldea, and lived without rule and order like the beast of the field.

In the first year there made its appearance, from a part of the Erythræan sea which bordered upon Babylonia, an animal endowed with reason, who was called Oannes. (According to the account of Apollodorus) the whole body of the animal was like that of a fish; and had under a fish's head another head, and also feet below, similar to those of a man, subjoined to the fish's tail. His voice too, and language, was articulate and human, and a representation of him is preserved even to this day

This Being in the day-time used to converse with men, but took no food at that season; and he gave them an insight into letters and sciences, and every kind of art. He taught them to construct houses, to found temples, to compile laws, and explained to them the principles of

ιδρυσεις, και νομων εισηγησεις,
και γεωμετριαν διδασκειν, και
στερματα, και καρπων συνα-
γωγας ὑποδεικνυειν, και συν-
ολως παντα τα προς ἡμερωσιν
ανηκοντα βιον παραδιδοναι τοις
ανθρωποις. απο δε του χρονου
εκεινου ουδεν αλλο περισσον
εὑρεθηναι. του δε ἡλιου δυναν-
τος το ζωον τουτοιι Ωαννην
διναι παλιν εις την θαλασσαν,
και τας νυκτας εκει διαιτασθαι
ειναι γαρ αυτον αμφιβιον

'Ὑστερον δε φανηναι και
ἑτερα ζωα ὁμοια τουτων, περι
ὡν εν τη των βασιλεων ανα-
γραφη (φησιν) δηλωσειν

Τον δε Ωαννην περι γενεας
και πολιτειας γραψαι, και
παραδουναι τονδε τον λογον τοις
ανθρωποις

" Γενεσθαι" φησι " χρονον,
εν ᾧ το παν σκοτος και ὑδωρ
ειναι, και εν τουτοις ζωα τερα-
τωδη, και ειδιφυεις τας ιδεας
εχοντα ζωογονεισθαι. ανθρωπους γαρ διπτερους γενηθηναι,
ενιους δε και τετραπτερους, και
διπροσωπους· και σωμα μεν
εχοντας ἑν, κεφαλας δε δυο,
ανδρειαν τε και γυναικειαν,
και αιδοια τε διττα, αρρεν και
θηλυ και ἑτερους ανθρωπους,
τους μεν αιγων σκελη και
κερατα εχοντας, τους δε ἱππο-

geometrical knowledge. He made them distinguish the seeds of the earth, and shewed them how to collect fruits; in short, he instructed them in every thing which could tend to soften manners and humanize mankind From that time, so universal were his instructions, nothing has been added material by way of improvement. When the sun set, it was the custom of this Being to plunge again into the sea, and abide all night in the deep; for he was amphibious.

After this there appeared other animals like Oannes, of which Berossus promises to give an account when he comes to the history of the kings.

Moreover Oannes wrote concerning the generation of mankind; of their different ways of life, and of their civil polity; and the following is the purport of what he said:

" There was a time in which there was nothing but darkness and an abyss of waters, wherein resided most hideous beings, which were produced of a two-fold principle. Men appeared with two wings, some with four and with two faces. They had one body but two heads, the one of a man, the other of a woman. They were likewise in their several organs both male and female Other human figures were to be seen with the legs and horns of goats. Some had horses' feet: others had the limbs of a horse ποδας, τους δε τα οπισω μεν μερη ίππων, τα δε εμπροσθεν ανθρωπων, οίς ίπποκενταυρους την ιδεαν ειναι. ζωογονηθηναι δε και ταυρους ανθρωπων κεφαλας εχοντας και κυνας τετρασωματους, ουρας ιχθυος εκ των οπισθεν μερων εχοντας, και ίππους κυνοκεφαλους, και ανθρωπους, και έτερα ζωα κεφαλας μεν και σωματα ίππων εχοντα, ουρας δε ιχθυων και αλλα δε ζωα παντοδαπων θηριων μορφας εχοντα. προς δε τουτοις, ιχθυας, και έρπετα, και οφεις, και αλλα ζωα πλειονα θαλασσα και παρηλλαγμενα τας οψεις αλληλων εχοντα· ών και τας εικονας εν τω του Βηλου ναω ανακεισθαι

" Αρχειν δε τουτων παντων γυναικα ή ονομα Ομορωκα ειναι δε τουτο Χαλδαιστι μεν Θαλατθ, Ἑλληνιστι δε μεθερμηνευεται θαλασσα, κατα δε ισοψηφον σεληνη· ούτως δε των όλων συνεστηκοτων, επανελθοντα Βηλον σχισαι την γυναικα μεσην, και το μεν ήμισυ αυτης ποιησαι γην, το δε αλλο ήμισυ ουρανον, και τα έν αυτη ζωα αφανισαι αλληγορικως δε (φησιν) τουτο μεν φυσιολογεισθαι. ύγρου γαρ οντος του παντος, και ζωων εν αυτω γεγενημενων, τουτον τον

behind, but before were fashioned like men, resembling hippocentaurs. Bulls likewise bred there with the heads of men, and dogs with fourfold bodies, and the tails of fishes. Also horses with the heads of dogs. men too and other animals, with the heads and bodies of horses and the tails of fishes. In short, there were creatures with the limbs of every species of animals Add to these fishes, reptiles, serpents, with other wonderful animals, which assumed each other's shape and countenance. Of all these were preserved delineations in the temple of Belus at Babylon.

" The person, who was supposed to have presided over them, was a woman named Omoroca ; which in the Chaldaic language is Thalatth ; which the Greeks express Thalassa, the sea: but according to the most true computation, it is equivalent to Selene, the moon All things being in this situation, Belus came, and cut the woman asunder · and out of one half of her he formed the earth, and of the other half the heavens, and at the same time destroyed the animals in the abyss. All this (he says) was an allegorical description of nature. For the whole universe consisting of

Θεον αφελειν την έαυτου κεφαλην, και το ῥυεν αἱμα τους
αλλους θεους φιρασθαι τη γη,
και διαπλασαι τοις ανθρωποις·
δια νοερους τε ειναι, και φρονη-
σεως θειας μετεχειν το· δε
Βηλον, ὁν Δια μεθερμηνευουσι,
μεσον τεμνοντα το σκοτος χω-
ρισαι γην και ουρανον απ'
αλληλων, και διαταξαι τον
κοσμον· τα δε ζωα ουκ ενεγ-
κοντα την του φωτος δυναμι·
φθαρηναι. ιδοντα δε τον Βηλον χωραν ερημον και καρπο-
φορον, κελευσαι ἑνι —ων θεων
την κεφαλην αφελοντι έαυτου
τῳ απορῥιεντι αἱματι φιρασαι
την γην, και διαπλασαι ανθρωπους, και θηρια τα δυναμενα
τον αερα φερειν· αποτελεσαι
δε τον Βηλον, και αστρα, και
ήλιον, και σεληνην, και τους
πεντε πλανητας "

(Εν δε τη δευτερᾳ τοις δεκα
βασιλεις των Χαλδαιων, και
τον χρονον της βασιλειας αυτων, σαρους έκατον εικοσι,
ήτοι ετων μυριαδας τεσσαρακοντα τρεις, και δυο χιλιαδας,
έως του κατανλυσμου. λεγει
γαρ ὁ αυτος Αλεξανδρος, ὡς
απο της γραφης των Χαλδαιων
αυθις παρακατιων απο εννατου

moisture, and animals being continually generated therein; the deity
(Belus) above-mentioned cut off his
own head upon which the other
gods mixed the blood, as it gushed
out, with the earth; and from thence
men were formed On this account
it is that they are rational, and partake of divine knowledge This Belus, whom men call Dis, divided the
darkness, and separated the Heavens
from the Earth, and reduced the
universe to order. But the animals
so lately created, not being able to
bear the prevalence of light, died.
Belus upon this, seeing a vast space
quite uninhabited, though by nature
very fruitful, ordered one of the gods
to take off his head, and when it
was taken off, they were to mix the
blood with the soil of the earth, and
from thence to form other men and
animals, which should be capable of
bearing the light Belus also formed
the stars, and the sun, and the moon,
together with the five planets.

(In the second book was the history
of the ten kings of the Chaldeans,
and the periods of each reign, which
consisted collectively of an hundred
and twenty sari, or four hundred and
thirty-two thousand years, reaching
to the time of the Deluge. For Alexander, as from the writings of the
Chaldæans, enumerating the kings
from the ninth Ardates to Xisuthrus,

βασιλεως Αρδατου επι τον
δεκατον λεγομενον παρ' αυτοις
Ξισουθρον, ούτας.)

Αρδατου δε τελευτησαντος
τον υίον αυτου Ξισουθρον βασιλευσαι σαρους οκτωκαιδεκα·
επι τουτου μεγαν κατακλυσμον γενεσθαι. αναγραφεσθαι
δε τον λογον ούτως τον Κρονον
αυτω κατα τον ύπνον επισ-
ταντα φαναι, μηνος Δαισια
πεμπτη και δεκατη τους
ανθρωπους ύπο κατακλυσμου
φθαρησεσθαι κελευσαι ουν
δια γραμματων παντων αρχας
και μεσα και τελετας ορυξ-
αντα θειναι εν πολει ήλιου
Σιππαροις, και ναυπηγησαμενον
σκαφος εμβηναι μετα των συγ-
γενων και αναγκαιων φιλων
ενθεσθαι δε βρωματα και πο-
ματα, εμβλειν δε και ζωα
πτηνα και τετραποδα, και
παντα ευτρεπισαμενον, πλειν
ερωτωμενον δε που πλει; φαναι,
προς τους Θεους· ευξαμενον ανθρωποις αγαθα γενεσθαι. τωδ'
ου παρακουσαντα, ναυπηγη-
σαντα σκαφος, το μεν μηκος
σταδιων πεντε, το δε πλατος
ςαδιων δυο τα δε συνταχθεντα
παντα συνθεσθαι, και γυναικα,
και τεκνα, και τους αναγκαιους
φιλους εμβιβασαι γενομενοι
δε του κατακλυσμου, και ευθεως ληξαντος· των ορνεων τινα

who is called by them the tenth,
proceeds in this manner.)

After the death of Ardates, his
son Xisuthrus succeeded, and reigned
eighteen sari In his time happened
the great Deluge; the history of which
is given in this manner The Deity,
Cronus, appeared to him in a vision,
and gave him notice that upon the
fifteenth day of the month Dæsia
there would be a flood, by which
mankind would be destroyed. He
therefore enjoined him to commit to
writing a history of the beginning,
procedure, and final conclusion of all
things, down to the present term;
and to bury these accounts securely
in the city of the Sun at Sippara;
and to build a vessel, and to take
with him into it his friends and re-
lations, and to convey on board
every thing necessary to sustain life,
and to take in also all species
of animals, that either fly or rove
upon the earth; and trust himself
to the deep. Having asked the
Deity, whither he was to sail?
he was answered, " To the Gods."
upon which he offered up a prayer for
the good of mankind. And he obeyed
the divine admonition: and built a
vessel five stadia in length, and in
breadth two Into this he put every
thing which he had got ready, and
last of all conveyed into it his wife,

τον Ξισουθρον αφιεναι. τα δε
ου τροφην ευροντα ουτε τοπον
όπου ναθισαι, παλιν ελθειν εις
το πλοιον. τον δε Ξισουθρον
παλιν μετα τινας ήμερας αφιεναι τα ορνεα· ταυτα δε παλιν
εις την ναυν ελθειν τους ποδας
πεπηλωμενους εχοντα· το δε
τριτον αφεθεντα, ουκ ετι ελθειν εις το πλοιον. τον δε Ξισουθρον εννοηθηναι γην ασαπε-
φηνεναι· διελοντα τε των του
πλοιου ραφων μερος τι, και
ιδοντα προσωκειλαν το πλοιον
ορει τινι, εκδηναι μετα της
γυναικος, και της θυγατρος,
και του κυβερνητου· προσκυνη-
σαντα την γην, και βωμον
ιδρυσαμενον, και θυσιασαντα
τοις θεοις, γενεσθαι μετα των
εκβαντων του πλοιου αφανη.
τους δε ὑπομειναντας εν τω
πλοιω, μη εισπορευομενων
των περι τον Ξισουθρον, εκ-
βαντας ζητειν αυτον επι ονοματος βοωντας. τον δε Ξισουθρον αυτον μεν αυτοις ουκ ετι
οφθηναι· φωνην δε εκ του αερος
γενεσθαι, κελευουσαν, ώς δεον
αυτους ειναι θεοσεβεις, και
παρ' αυτων δια την ευσεβειαν
πορευεσθαι μετα των θεων
οινησοντα. της δε αυτης τιμης
και την γυναικα αυτου, και
την θυγατερα, και τον κυβερ-
νητην μετεσχηνεναι. ειπεν τε

children, and friends. After the flood
had been upon the earth, and was in
time abated, Xisuthrus sent out some
birds from the vessel; which not
finding any food, nor any place to
rest their feet, returned to him again.
After an interval of some days, he
sent them forth a second time; and
they now returned with their feet
tinged with mud. He made a trial
a third time with these birds; but
they returned to him no more: from
whence he formed a judgment, that
the surface of the earth was now
above the waters. Having therefore
made an opening in the vessel, and
finding upon looking out, that the
vessel was driven to the side of a
mountain, he immediately quitted it,
being attended by his wife, his daughter, and the pilot. Xisuthrus immediately paid his adoration to the
earth: and having constructed an
altar, offered sacrifices to the gods.
These things being duly performed,
both Xisuthrus and those who came
out of the vessel with him, disappeared. They, who remained in the
vessel, finding that the others did
not return, came out with many
lamentations, and called continually
on the name of Xisuthrus. Him they
saw no more; but they could distinguish his voice in the air, and could
hear him admonish them to pay due
regard to the gods; and likewise

αυτοις· ότι ελευσονται παλιν εις Βαϐυλωνα, και ως ειμαρται αυτοις, εκ Σιππαρων ανελομενοις τα γραμματα διαδουναι τοις ανθρωποις· και ότι όπου εισιν, ή χωρα Αρμενιας εστιν· τους δε ακουσαντας αυτα Θυσαι τε τοις Θεοις, και περιξι πορευθηναι εις Βαϐυλωνα

inform them that it was upon account of his piety that he was translated to live with the gods; that his wife and daughter, with the pilot, had obtained the same honour. To this he added that he would have them make the best of their way to Babylonia, and search for the writings at Sippara, which were to be made known to all mankind: and that the place where they then were was the land of Armenia. The remainder having heard these words, offered sacrifices to the gods; and taking a circuit, journeyed towards Babylonia

Του δε πλοιου τουτου κατακλασθεντος εν τη Αρμενια ετ. μερος τι αυτου εν τοις Κορκυραιων ορεσι της Αρμενιας διαμενειν, και τινας απο του πλοιου κομιζειν αποξυοντας ασφαλτον, χρασθαι δε αυτην προς τους αποτροπιασμους. ελθοντας ουν τουτους εις Βαϐυλωνα, τατε εκ Σιππαρων γραμματα ανορυξαι, και πολεις πολλας κτιζοντας, και ιερα ανιδρισαμενους, παλιν επινισαι την Βαϐυλωνα

The vessel being thus stranded in Armenia, some part of it yet remains in the Corcyræan mountains in Armenia; and the people scrape off the bitumen, with which it had been outwardly coated, and make use of it by way of an alexipharmic and amulet. In this manner they returned to Babylon; and having found the writings at Sippara, they set about building cities, and erecting temples: and Babylon was thus inhabited again —*Syncel. Chron* 28.—*Euseb Chron.* 5. 8.

OF ABRAHAM.

Μετα τον κατακλυσμον δεκατη γενεα, παρα Χαλδαιοις τις ην δικαιος ανηρ, και μεγας, και τα ουρανια εμπειρος.

After the deluge, in the tenth generation, was a certain man among the Chaldæans renowned for his justice and great exploits, and for his skill in the celestial sciences. — *Euseb Præp Evan.* lib. 9.

OF NABONASAR

Απο δε Ναβονασαρου τους χρονους της των αστερων κινησεως Χαλδαιοι ηκριβωσαν, και απο Χαλδαιων οἱ παρ' Ελλησι μαθηματικοι λαβοντες πειδαν Ναβονασαρος συναγαγων τας πραξεις των προ αυτου βασιλεων, ηφανισεν, οπως απ' αυτου ἡ καταριθμησις γινεται των Χαλδαιων βασιλεων.

From the reign of Nabonasar only are the Chaldæans (from whom the Greek mathematicians copy) accurately acquainted with the heavenly motions for Nabonasar collected all the mementos of the kings prior to himself, and destroyed them, that the enumeration of the Chaldæan kings might commence with him.— *Syncel Chron.* 207.

OF THE DESTRUCTION OF THE JEWISH TEMPLE

Τινα τροπον πεμψας επι την Αιγυπτον και επι την ἡμετεραν γην τον υἱον τον ἑαυτου Ναβουχοδονοσορον μετα πολλης δυναμεως, επειδηπερ αφεστωτας αυτοις επυθετο, παντων εκρατησε, και τον ναον ενεπρησε τον εν Ἱεροσολυμοις,

He (Nabopollasar) sent his son Nabuchodonosor with a great army against Egypt, and against Judea, upon his being informed that they had revolted from him, and by that means he subdued them all, and set fire to the temple that was at Jerusalem; and removed our people entirely out

ὅλας τε παντα τον παρ' ἡμων
λαον αναστησας, εις Βαβυλωνα μετωγισεν συνεβη δε και
την πολιν ερημωθηνα χρονον
ετων ἑβδομηνοντα, μεχρι νιρυ
του Περσων βασιλεας στρατη-
σα. δε (φησι) τον Βαβυλωνιον
Αιγυπτου, Συριας, Φινικης,
Αραβιας, παντας δε ὑπερβαλ-
λομενον ταις πραξεσι τους προ
αυτου Χαλδαιαν και Βαβυλωνιων βεβασιλενοτας.

of theu own country, and tiansferied
them to Babylon, and it happened
that oui city was desolate during the
interval of seventy years, until the
days of Cyrus king of Persia (He
then says, that) this Babylonian
king conquered Egypt, and Syria,
and Phœnicia, and Arabia, and ex-
ceeded in his exploits all that had
reigned before him in Babylon and
Chaldæa — *Joseph. contr Appion.*
lib. 1. c. 19

OF NEBUCHADNEZZAR

Ακουσας δε ὁ πατηρ αυτου
Ναβοπολλασαρος, ὅτι ὁ τεταγμενος σατραπης ε᾽ε Αιγυπτω
και τοις περι την Συριαν την
Κοιλην και την Φοινικην τοποις
αποστατης γεγονεν, ου δυνα-
μενος αυτος ετι κακοπαθειν,
συστησας τω υιω Ναβουχοδ-
ονοσορω οντι ετι εν ἡλικια μερη
τινα της δυναμεας, εξετεμψεν
επ' αυτον συμμιξας δε Να-
βουχοδονοσορος τω αποστατη,
και παραταξαμενος, αυτου τε
εκυριευσεν, και την χωραν εξ
αρχης ὑπο την αὑτου βασιλειαν
εποιησεν. τω δε πατρι αυτου
συνεβη Ναβοπολλασαρω, κατα
τουτον τον καιρον αρρας ησαντι,
εν τη Βαβυλανιων πολει μεταλ-
λαξαι τον βιον, ετη βεβασι-
λευκοτι εικοσιν εννεα

When Nabopollasar his (Nabu-
chodonosoi's) father, heard that the
governor, whom he had set over
Egypt, and the parts of Cœlesyria
and Phœnicia, had revolted, he was
unable to put up with his delinquencies
any longer, but committed certain parts
of his army to his son Nabuchodonosor, who was then but young, and sent
him against the rebel · and Nabuchodonosor fought with him, and
conquered him, and reduced the
country again under his dominion
And it happened that his father,
Nabopollasar, fell into a distemper at
this time, and died in the city of
Babylon, after he had reigned twenty-
nine years

F

Αισθομενος δε μετ' ου πολυ
την του πατρος πελευτην Ναβουχοδονοσορος, καταστησας
τα κατα την Αιγυπτον πραγματα και την λοιπην χωραν,
και τους αιχμαλωτους Ιουδαιων
τε και Φοινικων και Συρων
και των κατα την Αιγυπτον
εθνων συνταξας τισι των φιλων,
μετα βαριτατης δυναμεως και
της λοιπης ωφελειας ανακομι-
ζειν εις την Βαβυλωνιαν, αυτος
ορμησας ολιγοστος παρεγενετο
δια της ερημου εις Βαβυλωνα.
καταλαβων δε τα πραγματα
διοικουμενα υπο Χαλδαιων, και
διατηρουμενην την βασιλειαν
υπο του βελτιστου αυτων, κυ-
ριευσας εξ ολοκληρου της πατρικης αρχης, τοις μεν αιχμα-
λωτοις παραγενομενος συνεταξ-
εν αυτοις αποικιας εν τοις
επιτηδειοτατοις της Βαβυλωνιας τοποις αποδειξαι αυτος δε
απο των εκ του πολεμου λαφυ-
ρων, τοτε Βηλου ιερον και τα
λοιπα κοσμησας φιλοτιμως,
την τε υπαρχουσαν εξ αρχης
πολιν, και ετεραν εξωθεν προσ-
χαρισαμενος και ανακαινησας,
προς το μηκετι δυνασθαι τους
πολιορκουντα, τον ποταμον
αναστρεφοντας ετι την πολιν
κατασκευαζειν, υπερεβαλετο
τρεις μεν της ενδον πολεως
περιβολοις, τρεις δε της εξω

After a short time Nabuchodonosor, receiving the intelligence of his father's death, set the affairs of Egypt and the other countries, in order, and committed the captives he had taken from the Jews, and Phœnicians, and Syrians, and of the nations belonging to Egypt, to some of his friends, that they might conduct that part of the forces that had on heavy armour, with the rest of his baggage, to Babylonia, while he went in haste, with a few followers, across the desert to Babylon, where, when he was come, he found that affairs had been well conducted by the Chaldæans, and that the principal person among them had preserved the kingdom for him accordingly he now obtained possession of all his father's dominions And he ordered the captives to be distributed in colonies in the most proper places of Babylonia. and adorned the temple of Belus, and the other temples, in a sumptuous and pious manner, out of the spoils he had taken in this war He also rebuilt the old city, and added another to it on the outside, and so far restored Babylon, that none, who should besiege it afterwards, might have it in their power to divert the river, so as to facilitate an entrance into it and this he did by building three walls about the inner city, and three about the outer. Some of these walls he

τουτων, τους μεν εξ οπτης πλινθου και ασφαλτου, τοις δε εξ
αυτης της πλινθου. και τειχι-
σας αξιολογας την πολιν, και
τους πυλωνας κοσμησας ιερο-
πρεπως, προσγατεσνευανεν τοις
πατρικοις βασιλειοις ετερα
βασιλεια εχομενα ενειναν,
ὑπεραιροντα αναστημα και την
πολλην πολυτελειαν μακρα δ'
ισως εσται εαν τις εξηγηται,
πλην οντα γε εις ὑπερβολην
ὡς μεγαλα και ὑπερηφανα,
συνετελεσθη ἡμεραις δεκαπεν-
τε. εν δε τοις βασιλειοις τουτοις αναλημματα λιθινα ίψηλα
ανῳκοδομησας, και την οψιν
αποδους ὁμοιοτατην τοις ορεσι,
καταφυτευσας δενδρεσι παν-
τοδαποις εξειργασατο, και
κατασκευασας τον καλουμενον
κρεμαστον παραδεισον, δια το
την γυναικα αυτου επιθυμειν
της ορειας διαθεσεως, τεθραμ-
μενην εν τοις κατα την Μηδιαν
τοποις.

built of burnt brick and bitumen, and
some of brick only. When he had
thus admirably fortified the city with
walls, and had magnificently adorned
the gates, he added also a new palace
to those in which his forefathers had
dwelt, adjoining them, but exceed-
ing them in height, and in its great
splendor. It would perhaps require
too long a narration, if any one were
to describe it: however, as prodi-
giously large and magnificent as it
was, it was finished in fifteen days.
In this palace he erected very high
walks, supported by stone pillars;
and by planting what was called
a pensile paradise, and replenishing
it with all sorts of trees, he rendered
the prospect an exact resemblance
of a mountainous country This he
did to please his queen, because she
had been brought up in Media, and
was fond of a mountainous situation.
—Joseph. contr Appion. lib. 1. c. 19.
—Syncel Chron. 220.— Euseb Præp.
Evan. lib. 9.

OF THE CHALDÆAN KINGS AFTER NEBUCHADNEZZAR.

Ναβουχοδονοσορος μεν ουν
μετα το αρξασθαι του προει-
ρημενου τειχους, εμπεσων εις
αρρωστιαν, μετηλλαξατο τον
βιον, βεβασιλευκως ετη τεσ-

Nabuchodonosor, after he had be-
gun to build the abovementioned wall,
fell sick, and departed this life, when
he had reigned forty-three years;
whereupon his son Evilmerodachus

σαρακοντατρια της δε βασιλειας κυριος εγενετο ὁ υἱος
αυτου Ενειλμαραδωχος οὑτος
προστας των πραγματων ανο-
μως και ατελγως, επιβουλευθεις ὑπο του την αδελφην
εχοντος αιτοι Νηριγλισσοορου
ανηρεθη, βασιλευσας ετη δυο.

Μετα δε το αναιρεθηναι
τουτον, διαδεξαμενος την αρχχην
ὁ επιβουλευσας αυτῳ Νηρι-
γλισσοορος, εβασιλευσεν ετη
τεσσαρα

Τουτου υἱος Λαβοροσοαρχο-
δος εκυριευσε μεν της βασιλειας παις ων μηνας εννεα·
επιβουλευθεις δε, δια το πολλα
εμφαινειν κακοηθη, ὑπο των
φιλων απετυμπανισθη.

Απολομενου δε τουτου, συν-
ελθοντες οἱ επιβουλευσαντες
αυτῳ, κοινῃ την βασιλειαν
περιεθηκαν Ναβοννηδῳ τινι των
εν Βαβυλωνος, οντι εκ της
αυτης επισυστασεας επι τουτ-
του τα περι τον ποταμον τειχη
της Βαβυλωνιων πολεας, εξ
οπτης πλινθου και ασφαλτου
κατεκοσμηθη

Ουσης δε της βασιλειας
αυτου εν τῳ ἑπταικαιδεκατῳ
ετει, προεξεληλυθως Κυρος εκ
της Περσιδος μετα δυναμεως
πολλης, και καταστρεψαμενος
την λοιπην Ασιαν πασαν, ὡρ-

obtained the kingdom. He governed public affairs in an illegal and improper manner, and by means of a plot laid against him by Neriglissoorus, his sister's husband, was slain when he had reigned but two years

After his death Neriglissoorus, who had conspired against him, succeeded him in the kingdom, and reigned four years

His son Laborosoarchodus obtained the kingdom though he was but a child, and kept it nine months; but by reason of the evil practices he exhibited, a plot was laid against him by his friends, and he was tormented to death

After his death, the conspirators assembled, and by common consent put the crown upon the head of Nabonnedus, a man of Babylon, and one of the leaders of that insurrection. In his reign it was that the walls of the city of Babylon were curiously built with burnt brick and bitumen

But in the seventeenth year of his reign, Cyrus came out of Persia with a great army, and having conquered all the rest of Asia, he came hastily to Babylonia. When Nabonnedus perceived he was advancing to at-

μησεν επι της Βαβυλωνιας
αισθομενος δε Ναβοννηδος την
εφοδον αυτευ απαντησας μετα
της δυναμεως και παραταξ-
αμενος, ηττηθεις τη μαχη και
φυγων ολιγιστος, συνενεισθη
εις την Βορσιτπηλαν πολιν.
Κυρος δε Βαβυλωνα καταλα-
βομενος, και συνταξας τα εξω
της πολεως τειχη κατασκαψαι,
δια το λιαν αυτω πραγματι-
κην και δυσαλωτον φανηναι
την πολιν, ανεζευξεν επι Βορ-
σιππον, εκπολιορκησαν τον Να-
βοννηδον του δε Ναβοννηδοι ουχ
υπομειναντος την πολιορνιαν,
αλλ' εγχειρησαντος αυτον,
προτερον χρησαμενος Κυρος φι-
λανθρωπως, και δους οικητηριον
αυτω Καρμανιαν, εξεπεμψεν
εκ της Βαβυλωνιας. Ναβον-
νηδος μεν ουν, το λοιπον του
χρονου διαγενομενος εν εκεινη
τη χωρα, κατεστρεψε τον βιον

tack him, he assembled his forces and opposed him, but was defeated, and fled with a few of his attendants, and was shut up in the city Borsippus. Whereupon Cyrus took Babylon, and gave orders that the outer walls should be demolished, because the city had proved very troublesome to him, and difficult to take. He then marched to Borsippus, to besiege Nabonnedus, but as Nabonnedus delivered himself into his hands without holding out the place, he was at first kindly treated by Cyrus, who gave him an habitation in Carmania, but sent him out of Babylonia. Accordingly Nabonnedus spent the remainder of his time in that country, and there died.— *Joseph contr App* lib. 1. c. 20 — *Euseb Præp Evan* lib 10

OF THE FEAST OF SACEA

Βηρωσσος δε εν πρωτω Βα-
βυλωνιακων, τω Λωω, φησι,
μηνι εκκαιδεκατη αγεσθαι εορ-
την Σακεας προσαγορευομενην
εν Βαβυλωνι επι ημερας πεντε,
εν αις εθος ειναι αρχεσθαι
τους δεσποτας υπο των οικετων,

Berossus, in the first book of his Babylonian history, says; That in the eleventh month, called Loos, is celebrated in Babylon the feast of Sacea for five days, in which it is the custom that the masters should obey their domestics, one of whom is led

αφηγεισθαι τε της οικιας ἑνα round the house, clothed in a royal
αυτων ενδεδινο-α ϛολην ὁμοιαν garment, and him they call Zoganes.
τη βασιλικη, ὁν ϛαλεισθαι —*Athenæus*, lib. 14.
Ζωγανην.

MEGASTHENES:

FROM ABYDENUS.

OF NEBUCHADNEZZAR

ΑΒΥΔΗΝΟΣ εν τη Ασσυριων γραφη, Μεγασθενης δε φησι. Ναβουκοδροσορον Ἡρακλεος αλκιμωτερον γεγονοτα επι τε Λιβυην και Ιβηριην στρατευσαι· ταυτας δε χειρωσαμενον αποδασμον αυτεων εις τα δεξια του ποντου κατοικισαι Μετα δε λεγεται προς Χαλδαιων, ὡς αναβας επι τα βασιληϊα κατασχεθειη θεῳ ὁτεῳ δη φθεγξαμενος δε ειπεν οὑτως " Εγω Ναβουκοδροσορος, ω Βαβυλωνιοι, την μελλουσαν ὑμιν προαγγελλω συμφορην, την ουτε Βηλος εμος προγονος, ουτε βασιλεια Βηλτις αποτρεψαι μοιρας πεισαι σθενουσι ἡξει Περσης ἡμιονος τοισι ὑμετεροισι δαιμοσι χρεωμενος συμμαχοισιν· επαξει δε δουλοσυνην ὁ δη συναιτιος εσται Μηδης το Ασσυριον αυχημα ὡ, ειθε μιν προσθεν, η δουναι τους πολιητας, χαρυβδιν τινα η θαλασ-

ABYDENUS, in his history of the Assyrians, has preserved the following fragment of Megasthenes, who says. That Nabucodrosorus, having become more powerful than Heicules, invaded Libya and Iberia, and when he had rendered them tributary, he extended his conquests over the inhabitants of the shores upon the right of the sea It is moreover related by the Chaldæans, that as he went up into his palace he was possessed by some god, and he cried out and said · " Oh ! Babylonians, I, Nabucodrosorus, foretel unto you a calamity which must shortly come to pass, which neither Belus my ancestor, nor his queen Beltis, have power to persuade the Fates to turn away A Persian mule shall come, and by the assistance of your gods shall impose upon you the yoke of slavery : the author of which shall be a Mede, the foolish pride of Assyria. Before he should thus betray my sub-

σαν εισδεξαμενην αιστωσαι
προρριζον, η μιν αλλας οδους
στραφεντα φερεσθαι δια της
ερημου, ίνα ουτε αστεα, ουτε
πατος ανθρωπων, θηρες δε
νομον εχουσ., και ορνιθες πλα-
ζονται, εν τε πετρησι και χα-
ραδρησι μουνον αλωμενον· εμε
τε πριν ες νοον βαλεσθαι ταυτα, τελεος αμεινονος κυρησαι "

Ὁ μεν θεσπισας; παρα-
χρημα ηφανιστο· ὁ δε οἱ παις
Ευιλμαλουρουχος εβασιλευε, τον
δε ὁ γηδεστης απκτεινας Νη-
ριγλισαρης, λειπε παιδα, Λα-
βασσοαρατνον. τουτου δε απο-
θανοντος βιαιω μορω, Ναβαν-
νιδοχον αποδεικνυσι βασιλεα,
προσηκοντα οἱ ουδεν τω δε
Κυρος ἑλων Βαβυλωνα Καρ-
μανιης ἡγεμονιην δωρεεται

(Και περι του κτιται δε τον
Ναβουχοδονοσορ την Βαβυ-
λωνα, ὁ αυτος ταυτα γραφει)
λεγεται δε παντα μεν εξ αρχης ύδωρ ειναι, θαλασσαν
καλεομενην Βηλον δε σφεα
παυσαι, χωρην ἑκαστω απονει-
μαντα, και Βαβυλωνα τειχει
περιβαλειν· τω χρονω δε τω
ικνευμενω αφανισθηναι. τειχι-
σαι δε αυθις Ναβουχοδονοσορ,
το μεχρι της Μακεδονων αρχης διαμειναι εον χαλκοπυλον.
Και μεθ' ἑτερα επιλεγει, Να-

jects, Oh! that some sea or whirlpool
might receive him, and his memory
be blotted out for ever, or that he
might be cast out to wander through
some desert, where there are neither
cities nor the trace of men, a solitary
exile among rocks and caverns, where
beasts and birds alone abide But
for me, before he shall have conceived
these mischiefs in his mind, a hap-
pier end will be provided."

When he had thus prophesied, he
expired. and was succeeded by his
son Evilmaluruchus, who was slain
by his kinsman Neriglisares: and
Neriglisares left Labassoarascus his
son· and when he also had suffered
death by violence, they made Naban-
nidochus king, being no relation to the
royal race, and in his reign Cyrus
took Babylon, and granted him a
principality in Carmania

And concerning the rebuilding of
Babylon by Nabuchodonosor, he
writes thus. It is said that from the
beginning all things were water, called
the sea (Thalatth?) that Belus caused
this state of things to cease, and appointed to each its proper place·
and he surrounded Babylon with a
wall· but in process of time this
wall disappeared and Nabuchodonosor walled it in again, and it remained so with its brazen gates until
the time of the Macedonian conquest
And after other things he says Na-

βουχοδονοσορος δε διαδεξαμενος την αρχην, Βαβυλωνα μεν ετειχισε τριπλω περιβολω, εν πεντεκαιδεκα ἡμερησι, τον δε Ἀρμακαλην ποταμον εξηγαγεν, εοντα νερας Ευφρητεω, τον τε Ἀγρανανον ὑπερ δε της Στ-παρηναν πολιος λαιναν ορυξαμενος, περιμετρον μεν τεσσαρακουτα παρασαγ͵εων, βαθος δ᾽ οργυιαν εικοσι, πυλας επεστησεν, τας ανοιγουντες αρδεσιον το πεδιον· καλεοισι δ᾽ αυτας εχετογνωμονας επετειχισε δε και της Ερυθρης θαλασσης την επικλυσιν, και Τερηδονα πολιν εντισεν, κατα τας Αραβων εισβολας· τα τε βασιληια δενδροις ησνησε, κρημματτιας παραδεισους ονοματας

buchodonosor having succeeded to the kingdom, built the walls of Babylon in a triple circuit in fifteen days ; and he turned the river Armacale, a branch of the Euphrates, and the Acracanus and above the city of Sippara he dug a receptacle for the waters, whose perimeter was forty parasangs, and whose depth was twenty cubits ; and he placed gates at the entrance thereof, by opening which they irrigated the plains, and these they call Echetognomones (sluices.) and he constructed dykes against the irruptions of the Erythræan sea, and built the city of Teredon against the incursions of the Arabs, and he adorned the palace with trees, calling them hanging gardens —*Euseb Prap Evan* lib 10 —*Euseb Chron.* 49.

THE FRAGMENTS

OF

THE EGYPTIAN HISTORIES:

CONTAINING

THE HERMETIC CREED;
THE OLD CHRONICLE;
THE REMAINS OF MANETHO;
AND
THE LATERCULUS OF ERATOSTHENES.

THE HERMETIC CREED:

ΠΡΟ των οντως οντων, και των ὁλων αρχων, ες-ι θεος εἱς, πρωτος και του πρωτου Θεου και βασιλεως, ακινητος εν μονοτητι της ἑαυτου ενοτητος μενων, ουτε γαρ νοητον αυτω επιπλεκεται, ουτε αλλο τι. Παραδειγμα δε ἱδρυται του αυτου πατρος, αυτογονου, και μονοπατορος Θεου, του οντως αγαθου. Μειζον γαρ τε και πρωτον, και πηγη των παντων, και πυθμην των νοουμενων πρωτων ειδων οντων. Απο δε του ἑνος τουτου, ὁ αυταρχης Θεος ἑαυτον εξελαμψε· διο και αυτοπατωρ και αιταρχης. Αρχη γαρ αυτος και Θεος Θεων. Μονας εκ του ἑνος, προ ουσιας, και Αρχη της ουσιας· απ' αυτου γαρ ἡ ουσιοτης και ἡ ουσια· διο και νοηταρχης προσαγορευεται. Αυται μεν ουν εισιν αρχαι πρεσβυταται

BEFORE all things that really exist, and before the beginning of all time, there is one God, prior to the first God, and ruler of the world, remaining immoveable in the solitude of his unity; for neither is intelligence immixed with him, nor any other thing. He is the exemplar of himself; the Father, the self-begotten God, who is the only Father, and is truly good For he is the greatest and the first, the fountain of all things and the root of all primary intellectual forms But out of this one, the God that is self-sufficient shone forth of himself: for which reason he is the father of himself, and all-sufficient. for he is the beginning and the God of gods. He is unity from the only one; before essence, and yet he is the beginning of essence, for from him is entity and essence; on which account he is celebrated as the prince of intelli-

παντων, ὡς Ἑρμης προ των αιθεριων και εμπυριων Θεων προσταττει και των επου-ρανιων.

gence. These are the most ancient principles of all things, which Hermes places first in order, before the ethereal, empyrean, and celestial deities. —*Jamblichus.*

THE OLD EGYPTIAN CHRONICLE.

ΦΕΡΕΤΑΙ γαρ Αιγυπτιοις πα-
λαιον τι χρονογραφειον περιεχον
λ'. δυναϛειων εν γενεαις παλιν
ριγ'. χρονων απειρων, εν μυριασι, τρισι, και ‚ϛφλε'. πρωτον
μεν των Αιριτων, δευτερον δε
των Μεστραιων, τριτον δε Αι-
γυπτιων· ούτω πως επι λεξεως
εχον

'Ηφαιστου χρονος ουν εστιν·
δια το νυκτος και ημερας
αυτον φαινειν.

'Ηλιος 'Ηφαιστου εβασι-
λευσεν ετων μυριαδας τρεις.

Επειτα Κρονος (φησι) και
οἱ λοιποι παντες θεοι δωδεκα
εβασιλευσεν ετη, ‚γ πηπδ'.

Επειτα ἡμιθεοι βασιλεις
οκτω ετη σιζ'.

Και μετ' αυτους γενεαι ιε'.
Κυνικου κυκλου ανεγραφησαν
εν ετεσι υμγ'.

Ειτα Τανιτων ις'. δυναϛ-
τεια, γενεων η'. ετων ρϟ'.

AMONG the Egyptians there is a certain tablet called the Old Chronicle, containing thirty dynasties in 113 descents, during the long period of 36525 years. The first series of princes was that of the Auritæ; the second was that of the Mestræans, the third of Egyptians. The Chronicle runs as follows:

To Hephæstus is assigned no time, as he is apparent both by night and day.

Helius the son of Hephæstus reigned three myriads of years.

Then Cronus and the other twelve divinities reigned 3984 years.

Next in order are the demigods, in number eight, who reigned 217 years.

After these are enumerated 15 generations of the Cynic circle, which take up 443 years.

The 16th Dynasty is of the Tanites, eight kings, which lasted 190 years.

Προς οἷς ιζ´ δυναςεια Μεμφιτων, γενεων δ´. ετων ργ´.

17th Memphites,   4 ın descent,
103 years.

Μεθ᾽ οὑς ιη´. δυναςεια Μεμφιτων, γενεων ιδ´. ετων τμη´

18th Memphıtes,   14 ın descent,
348 years.

Επειτα ιθ´ δυναστεια Διοσπολιτων, γενεων ε´. ετων ρϟδ´.

19th Dıospolıtes,   5 ın descent,
194 years.

Εἰτα εικοστη δυναστεια
Διοσπολιταν, γενεων η´. ετων
σκη´.

20th Dıospolıtes,   8 ın descent,
228 yeaıs

Επειτα κα´. δυναστεια Τα-
νιταν, γενεων ϛ´. ετων ρκα´.

21st Tanıtes,   .   6 ın descent,
121 years.

Εἰτα κβ´. δυναστεια Τανι-
των, γενεων γ´. ετων μη´

22nd Tanıtes,   .   3 in descent,
48 years.

κγ´ δυναστεια Δ.οσπολιτων,
γενεων β´. ετων ιϛ´.

23rd Dıospolıtes,   2 ın descent,
19 years.

Εἰτα κδ´ δυναστεια Σαιτων,
γενεων γ´ εταν μδ´.

24th Saıtes,   .   3 ın descent,
44 years

Προς οἷς κε´ δυναστεια Αι-
θιοπαν, γενεων γ´. ετων μδ´.

25th Ethıopıans,   3 ın descent,
44 yeaıs.

Μεθ᾽ οὑς ιϛ´. δυναστεια
Μεμφιτων, γενεων ζ´. εταν ροζ´.

26th Memphıtes,   7 ın descent,
177 years.

Και μετα τουτους κζ´. Περσων ε´. εταν ρνδ

27th Persıans   .   5 ın descent,
124 years

νη´.

28th

Επειτα νθ´. δυναστεια Τα-
νιτων, γενεων, ετων λϛ´.

29th Tanıtes,   .   ın descent,
39 years.

Και επι πασαις λ´ δυνασ-
τεια Τανιτοι ἑνος, ετων ιη´.

30th a Tanıte,   .   1 ın descent,
18 yeaıs.

Τα παντα ὁμου των λ´.
δυναστειων ετη μυριαδας γ´.
λαι ͵ϛφκε´.

In all, 30 Dynastıes, and 36525
years.—*Syncel. Chron* 51.—*Euseb
Chron.* 6.

MANETHO:

THE EPISTLE OF MANETHO, THE SEBENNYTE, TO PTOLEMY PHILADELPHUS.

ΒΑΣΙΛΕΙ μεγαλῳ Πτολεμαιῳ Φιλαδελφῳ σεβαστῳ, Μανεθω αρχιερευς και γραμματευς των κατ' Αιγυπτον ἱερων αδυτων, γενει Σεβεννυτης ὑπαρχων, Ἡλιουπολιτης, τῳ δεσποτη μου Πτολεμαιῳ Χαιρειν.

Ἡμας δει λογιζεσθαι, μεγιστε βασιλευ, ωερι ωαντων ὡν εαν βουλη ἡμας εξετασαι ωραγματων· επιζητουντι σοι ωερι των μελλοντων τῳ κοσμῳ γιγνεσθαι καθετος καλευσας μοι ωεριφανησεται σοι ἁ εμαθον ἱερα βιβλια γραφεντα ὑπο των προπατορος τρισμεγιστου Ἑρμου, Ερῥωσο μοι, Δεσποτα μου Βασιλευ.

To the great and august king Ptolemy Philadelphus: Manetho, the high priest and scribe of the sacred adyta in Egypt, being by birth a Sebennyte and a citizen of Heliopolis, to his sovereign Ptolemy, humbly greeting:

It is right for us, most mighty king, to pay due attention to all things which it is your pleasure we should take into consideration. In answer then to your inquiries concerning the things which shall come to pass in the world, I shall, according to your commands, lay before you what I have gathered from the sacred books written by Hermes Trismegistus, our forefather. Farewell, my prince and sovereign. — *Syncel. Chron* 40.— *Euseb. Chron.* 6.

THE EGYPTIAN DYNASTIES.

THE DYNASTY OF THE DEMIGODS.

Αιγυπτιων α'. εβασιλευσεν Ἡφαιστος ετη ψκδ'. ἡμισυ και τεσσαρας ἡμερας.

The 1st of the Egyptian kings was Hephæstus, who reigned 724 years and a half and 4 days.

Αιγυπτιων β'. εβασιλευσεν Ἡλιος Ἡφαιστου ετη πς'

The 2nd was Helius, the son of Hephæstus, 86 years.

Αιγυπτιων γ'. εβασιλευσεν Αγαθοδαιμων ετη νς'. και ἡμισυ και δεκα ἡμερας.

3rd, Agathodæmon, who reigned 56 and a half and ten days.

Αιγυπτιων δ'. εβασιλευσεν Κρονος ετη μ'. και ημισυ.

4th, Cronus, 40 and a half years.

Αιγυπτιων ε'. εβασιλευσεν Οσιρις και Ισις ετη λε'.

5th, Osiris and Isis, 35 years.

Αιγυπτιων ς'. εβασιλευσεν ετη

6th,   .   .   .   years.

Αιγυπτιων ζ'. εβασιλευσεν Τυφων ετη κθ'.

7th, Typhon, 29 years.

Αιγυπτιων η'. εβασιλευσεν Ὡρος ἡμιθεος ετη κε'.

8th, Horus, the demigod, 25 years.

Αιγυπτιων θ'. εβασιλευσεν Αρης ἡμιθεος ετη κγ'.

9th, Ares, the demigod, 23 years.

Αιγυπτιων ι'. εβασιλευσεν Ανουβις ἡμιθεος ετη ιζ'.

10th, Anubis, the demigod, 17 years.

Αιγυπτιων ια'. εβασιλευσεν Ἡρακλης ἡμιθεος ετη ιε'.

11th, Heracles, the demigod, 15 years.

Αιγυπτιων ιβ' εβασιλευσεν Απολλω ἡμιθεος ετη κε'

12th, Apollo, the demigod, 25 years.

Αιγυπτιων ιγ'. εβασιλευσεν
Αμμων ήμιθεος ετη λ'.

13th, Ammon, the demigod, 30 years

Αιγυπτιων ιδ'. εβασιλευσεν
Τιθοης ήμιθεος ετη κζ'.

14th, Tithoes, the demigod, 27 years.

Αιγυπτιων ιε' εβασιλευσεν
Σωσος ήμιθεος ετη λβ'.

15th, Sosus, the demigod, 32 years.

Αιγυπτιων ις'. εβασιλευσεν
Ζευς ήμιθεος ετη ʎ'.

16th, Zeus, the demigod, 20 years.—
Syncel. Chron. 19.—*Euseb. Chron.* 7.

THE EGYPTIAN DYNASTIES AFTER THE DELUGE.

THE FIRST DYNASTY

α'. Μετα νεκυας τους ήμιθεους πρωτη βασιλεια καταριθμειται βασιλεων οκτω, ών πρωτος Μηνης Θεινιτης εβασιλευσεν ετη ξβ'. ὁς ὑπο Ἱπποποταμου διαπραγεις διεφθαρη

1. After the dead demigods the first dynasty consisted of eight kings, of whom the first was Menes the Thinite; he reigned 62 years, and perished by a wound received from an hippopotamus.

β'. Αθωθις (Αθωσθις)* υἱος ετη νζ'. ὁ τα εν Μεμφει βασιλεια οικοδομησας· οὐ φερονται βιβλοι ανατομικαι, ιατρος γαρ ην.

2. Athothis, his son, reigned 57 years; he built the palaces at Memphis, and left the anatomical books, for he was a physician.

γ' Κενκενης (Κερκενης) υἱος ετη λα'.

3 Cencenes, his son, reigned 31 years.

δ'. Ουενεφης (Ουενεφρης) υἱος ετη κγ'. εφ'. οὐ λιμος κατεσχεν την Αιγυπτον μεγας. οὑτος παρα Κωχωμην ηγειρε πυραμιδας.

4. Venephes, his son, reigned 23 years. In his time a great plague raged through Egypt. He raised the pyramids near Cochome.

ε'. Ουσαφαιδος (Ουσαφαης) υἱος ετη ʎ'.

5. Usaphædus, his son, reigned 20 years.

* The names and paragraphs contained between the parentheses are the variations which occur in Eusebius.

ς΄. Μιεβιδος (Νιεβης) υιος
ετη κς΄.

6. Miebidus, his son, 26 years.

ζ΄. Σεμεμψις (Σεμεμψης)
υιος ετη ιη΄. εφ΄ ου φθορα μεγιστη κατεσχεν την Αιγυπτον

7 Semempsis, his son, reigned 18 years. In his reign a terrible pestilence afflicted Egypt

η΄. Βιηναχης (Ουβιεντης)
υιος ετη κς΄

8. Bienaches, his son reigned 26 years.

Ομου ετη σνγ΄.

The whole number of years amounted to 253.

THE SECOND DYNASTY

Δευτερα δυναστεια Θεινι-
των βασιλεων εννεα ων.

Of nine Thinite kings.

α΄. Πρωτος Βοηθος (Βωχος)
ετη λη΄. εφ΄ ου χασμα κατα
Βουβαστον εγενετο, και απωλ-
οντο πολλοι.

1. Boethus the first reigned 38 years. During his reign a chasm of the earth opened near Bubastus, and many persons perished.

β΄. Καιαχως (Χοος) ετη
λθ΄ εφ΄ ου οι βοες Απις εν
Μεμφει, και Μηνευς εν Ἡλιου-
πολει, και ὁ Μενδησιος τραγος
ενομιθησαν ειναι θεοι.

2. Cæachos reigned 39 years. Under him the bulls Apis in Memphis, and Meneus in Heliopolis, and the Mendesian goat, were appointed to be gods.

γ΄ Βινωθρις (Βιοφις) ετη
μζ΄. εφ΄ ου εκριθη τας γυναικας
βασιλειας γερας εχειν.

3 Binothris reigned 47 years. In whose time it was judged that women might hold the imperial government.

δ΄. Τλας ετη .ζ΄.

4. Tlas reigned 17 years.

ε΄. Σεθενης ετη μα΄.

5. Sethenes reigned 41 years.

ς΄ Χοιρης ετη ιζ΄

6. Chæres 17 years.

ζ΄. Νεφερχερης ετη νε΄. εφ΄
ου μυθευεται τον Νειλον μελιτι
κεκραμμενον ἡμερας ἑνδεκα
ῥυηναι.

7, Nephercheres 25 years. In his time it is said the Nile flowed with honey during eleven days.

(η΄. Σεσαχρις ετη μη΄, ὁς
ὑψος ειχε πηχων ε΄. πλατος γ΄

(8. Sesochris 48 years, whose height was five cubits, and his breadth three.

θ'. Χενερης ετη λ'
Ομου ετη τβ')

9 Cheneres 30 years.
The whole number of years is 302.)

THE THIRD DYNASTY.

Τριτη δυναστεια Μεμφιτων βασιλεων εννεα· ὧν

α'. Νεχεροφης (Νεχερωχις) ετη κη'· εφ' οὗ Λιβυες απεστησαν Αιγυπτιων, και της σεληνης παρα λογον αυξηθεισης, δια δεος ἑαυτους παρεδοσαν

β'. Τοσορθρος (Σεσορθος) ετη λθ'. οὗτος Ασκληπιος Αιγυπτιος κατα την ιατρικην νενομισται, και την δια ξεςων λιθων οικοδομιαν εὑρατο, αλλα και γραφης επεμεληθη.

γ'. Τυρις ετη ζ'.
δ'. Μεσωχρις ετη ιζ'.
ε'. Σωιφις ετη ιϛ'.
ϛ' Τοσερτασις ετη ιθ'.
ζ'. Αχις ετη μβ'.
η'. Σιφουρις ετη λ'
θ'. Κερφερης ετη κϛ'.
Ομου εστιν σιδ'.

Of nine Memphite kings.

1. Necherophes reigned 28 years. In his time the Libyans revolted from the Egyptians, but on account of an unexpected increase of the moon they surrendered themselves for fear.

2. Tosorthrus reigned 29 years. He is called Asclepius by the Egyptians, for his medical knowledge. He built a house of hewn stones, and greatly patronized writing

3. Tyris reigned 7 years.
4. Mesochris 17 years.
5. Soiphis 16 years.
6. Tosertasis 19 years.
7. Achis 42 years.
8. Siphuris 30 years.
9. Cerpheres 26 years.
Altogether 214 years.

THE FOURTH DYNASTY.

Τεταρτη δυναστεια Μεμφιτων συγγενειας ἑτερας βασιλεις η'.

α'. Σωρις ετη κθ'.
β'. Σουφις ετη ξγ'. ὃς την

Of eight Memphite kings of a different race

1. Soris reigned 29 years.
2. Suphis reigned 63 years. He

μεγιστην ηγειρε πυραμιδα, ου- | built the largest pyramid . he was
τος δε και ὁ Περοπτης εις θεους | called also Peroptes, and was trans-
εγενετο και την ιεραν συνεγραφε | lated to the gods, and wrote the
βιβλον. | sacred book.

γ΄ Σουφις ετη ξς΄. 3. Suphis reigned 66 years
δ΄. Μενχερης ετη ξγ΄. 4. Mencheres 63 years.
ε΄. Ρατοισης ετη κε΄. 5. Ratœses 25 years.
ς΄. Βιχερης ετη κβ΄. 6. Bicheres 22 years.
ζ΄. Σεβερχερης ετη ζ΄. 7. Sebercheres 7 years.
η΄. Θαμφθις ετη θ΄. 8. Thampthis 9 years.
Ομου ετη σοδ΄. Altogether 274 years.

THE FIFTH DYNASTY

Πεμπτη δυναστεια βασι- | Of nine Elephantine kings.
λεων εξ Ελεφαντινης.

α΄. Ουσερχερις ετη κη΄. 1. Usercheris reigned 28 years.
β΄. Σεφρης ετη ιγ΄. 2. Sephres 13 years
γ΄. Νεφερχερης ετη κ΄. 3. Nephercheres 20 years.
δ΄ Σισιρις ετη ζ΄. 4. Sisiris 7 years.
ε΄. Χερης ετη κ΄ 5. Cheres 20 years.
ς΄ Ραθουρις ετη μδ΄. 6. Rathuris 44 years.
ζ΄. Μερχερης ετη θ΄. 7. Mercheres 9 years
η΄. Ταρχερης ετη μδ΄. 8. Taicheres 44 years.
θ΄. Οβνος ετη λγ΄. 9. Obnos 33 years
Ομου ετη σμη΄. Altogether 248 years.

THE SIXTH DYNASTY.

Ἑκτη δυναστεια βασιλεων | Of six Memphite kings
εξ Μεμφιτων.

α΄. Οθωης, (Θωης) ὁ, υπο | 1. Othoes, who was killed by his
δορυτων φορων ανηρεθη. | guards.

β΄. Φιος ετη νγ΄. 2. Phius reigned 53 years.

γ'. Μεθουσουφις ετη ζ'.

3. Methusuphis 7 years

δ'. Φιωψ (Αφιωψ) ἐξαετης αρξαμενος βασιλευειν. διεγενετο μεχρις ετων ρ'.

4. Phiops who began to reign at six years of age, and reigned till he had completed his hundredth year.

ε'. Μεντεσουφις ετος ἐν.

5. Mentesuphis reigned one year.

ς'. Νιτωκρις γενικωτατη, και ειμορφοτατη των κατ' αυτην γενομενη, ξανθη την χροιαν ἡ την τριτην ηγειρε πυραμιδα· εβασιλευσεν ετη ιβ'.

6. Nitocris, who was the most handsome woman of her time, of a dark complexion ; she built the third pyramid, and reigned 12 years

Ομου ετη σγ'.

Altogether 203 years.

THE SEVENTH DYNASTY.

Ἑβδομη δυναστεια Μεμφιτων βασιλεων ο'. οἱ εβασιλευσαν ἡμερας ο'.

Of seventy Memphite kings, who reigned 70 days.

THE EIGHTH DYNASTY.

Ογδοη δυναστεια Μεμφιτων βασιλεων κζ'. οἱ εβασιλευσαν ετη ρμς'.

Of twenty-seven Memphite kings, who reigned 146 years.

THE NINTH DYNASTY.

Εννατη δυναστεια Ἡρακλεωτικων βασιλεων ιθ' οἱ εβασιλευσαν ετη νθ' ὡν

Of nineteen Heracleotic kings, who reigned 409 years

Ὁ πρωτος Αχθοης δεινοτατος των προ αυτου γενομενος, τοις εν παση Αιγυπτω κακα ειργασατο, μανιᾳ περιεπεσεν, και ὑπο κρονοδειλου διεφθαρη.

1. The first was Achthoes, the worst of all his predecessors. He did much harm to all the inhabitants of Egypt, was seized with madness, and killed by a crocodile.

THE TENTH DYNASTY.

Δεκατη δυναστεια Ἡρα-
κλεωτικων βασιλεων ιθ'. οἱ
ἐβασιλευσαν ρπε'.

Of 19 Heracleotic kings, who
reigned 185 years

THE ELEVENTH DYNASTY.

Ἑνδεκατη δυναστεια Διοσ-
πολιτων βασιλεων ιϛ' οἱ ἐβασιλευσαν ετη μγ'. μεθ' οὑς
Αμμενεμης ετη ιϛ'.

Ομου βασιλεις, ρϟβ' ετη,
βτη'. ἡμερας ο'.

Of sixteen Diospolites kings, who
reigned 43 years.   Among whom
Ammenemes reigned 16 years.

The whole number of the above-
mentioned kings is 192, who reigned
during a space of 2308 years and
70 days — *Syncel Chron.* 54 to 59.
—*Euseb. Chron.* 14, 15.

THE SECOND BOOK OF MANETHO·

THE TWELFTH DYNASTY

ΔΩΔΕΚΑΤΗ δυναστεια Διοσ-
πολιτων βασιλεων έπτα.

Of seven Diospolite kings

α'. Γεσων Γωσης Αμμα-
νεμου (Σεσογχορις Αμμενεμου)
υίος ετη μς'.

1 Geson Goses the son of Ammanemes   He reigned 46 years

β'. Αμμανεμης (Αμμενε-
μης) ετη λη'. ός ύπο των ιδιων
εινουχων ανηρεθη

2. Ammanemes reigned 38 years
He was slain by his eunuchs

γ'. Σεσωστρις ετη μη' ός
άτασαν εχειρωσατο την Ασιαν
εν ελιαυτοις εννεα, και της
Ευρωπης τα μεχρι Θρακης
πανταχοσε μνημοσυνα εγειρας
της των εθνων κατασχεσεως
επι μεν τοις γενναιοις, ανδρων·
ετι δε τοις αγεννεσι, γυναικων
μορια ταις στηλαις εγχαρασ-
σων, ός ύπο Αιγυπτιων μετα
Οσιριν πρωτον νομισθηναι.

3 Sesostris 48 years   He conquered all Asia in nine years, and
Europe as far as Thrace, every where
erecting monuments of his conquests
of those nations, of men among nations who acted bravely, but among
the degenerate he erected figures of
women, engraving their follies upon
the pillars.   By the Egyptians he is
supposed to be the first after Osiris.

δ'. Λαχαρης (Λαβαρις) ετη
ή'. ός των εν Αρσενοιτη λαβυριν-
θον έαυτω ταφον κατεσκευ-
ασεν

4. Lachares 8 years, who built the
Labyrinth in Arsenoite as a tomb for
himself.

ε΄ Αμμερης ετη η΄   5. Ammeres 8 years
ς΄. Αμμενεμης ετη η΄.   6. Ammenemes 8 years.
ζ΄. Σκεμιοφρις αδελφη ετη δ΄. 7. Scemiophris, his sister, 4 years.
Ομου ετη ρξ΄.   Altogether 160 years.

THE THIRTEENTH DYNASTY

Τριςκαιδεκατη   δυναστεια   Of 60 Diospolite kings, who reigned
Διοσπολιτων βασιλεων ξ΄. οι   184 years.
εβασιλευσαν ρπδ΄ ετη.

Λειπει   The names are lost.

THE FOURTEENTH DYNASTY.

Is lost altogether.

THE FIFTEENTH DYNASTY

Πεντεδεκατη* ποιμενων   Of the Shepherds.

Ησαν δε Φοινικες ξενοι βα-   There were six foreign Phœnician
σιλεις ς΄. οι και Μεμφιν ειλον.   kings . they took Memphis, and
οι και εν τῳ Σεθροιτη νομῳ   built a city in the Sethroite nome,
πολιν εκτισαν, αφ᾽ ης ορμω-   from whence they made an inva-
μενοι Αιγυπτιους εχειρωσαντο,   sion, and conquered all Egypt, of
ὡν   whom

α΄ Σαιτης εβασιλευσεν ετη   1. Saites reigned 19 years, after
ιθ΄ αφ᾽ ου και ὁ Σαιτης νομος.   whom the Saite Nome is so called

β΄. Βνων (Βναν Αναν) ετη   2 Beon reigned 44 years.
μδ΄

γ΄. Παχναν (Αφωφις) ετη   3. Pachnan 61 years.
ξα΄.

δ΄. Στααν ετη ν΄.   4 Staan 50 years.

ε΄. Αρχλης (Αυχλης) ετη μθ΄.   5. Archles 49 years.

* This is the seventeenth according to Eusebius

ς'. Αφοϐις ετη ξα'.   6. Aphobis 61 years
Ομου ετη σπδ'.   Altogether 284 years.

THE SIXTEENTH DYNASTY.

'Εκκαιδεκατη δυναςεια ποι-   Of 32 Grecian shepherds, who
μενες 'Ελληνες βασιλεις λϐ'.   reigned 518 years.
εϐασιλευσαν ετη φιη'.

THE SEVENTEENTH DYNASTY.

'Επτακαιδεκατη δυναστεια   Consisted of 43 shepherd kings
ποιμενες αλλοι βασιλεις μγ'.   and 43 Theban Diospolites.
Και Θηϐαιοι Διοσπολιται μγ'.

Ομου οἱ ποιμενες, και οἱ   The Shepheids and Thebans reigned
Θηϐαιοι εϐασιλευσαν ετη ρνα'. altogether 151 years.

THE EIGHTEENTH DYNASTY

Οντωκαιδεκατη δυναστεια   Of sixteen Diospolite kings.
Διοσπολιταν βασιλεων ις' ὡν

α'. Πρωτος Αμως (Αμωσις   1. Amos
ετη κε')

β'. Χεϐρας (Χεϐρων)ετη ιγ'   2. Chebros 13 years.

γ'. Αμενωφθις (Αμμενουφος)   3 Amenophthis 24 years.
ετη νδ'

δ'. Αμερσις (Μιφρις) ετη   4. Amersis 22 years.
κϐ'.

ε'. Μισαφρις* ετη ιγ'.   5. Misaphris 13 years.

ς'. Μισφραγμουθωσις ετη   6. Misphragmathosis 26 years, in

---

* In the list of Eusebius the fifth is omitted, and the name of Χερρης inserted
between the thirteenth and fourteenth.

ϛ' εφ' οὗ ὁ επι Δεικαλιανος νατακλυσμος.

whose time happened the deluge of Deucalion

ζ'. Τουθμωσις ετη θ'.

7. Tuthmosis 9 years

η'. Αμενωφις ετη λα'. οὗτος εστιν ὁ Μεμνων ειναι νομιζομενος, και φθεγγομενος λιθος.

8. Amenophis 31 years. He is supposed to be Memnon, to whom the musical statue is erected.

θ'. Ὡρος ετη λζ'

9. Horus 37 years.

ι'. Αχερρης (Αχειχερσης) ετη λϛ'

10 Acherrhes 32 years.

ια'. Ραθως (Αθωρις) ετη ἑξ'

11 Rathos 6 years.

ιϐ'. Χεϐρης (Χενχερης) ετη ιϐ'.

12. Chebres 12 years.

ιγ'. Αχερρης (Αχερρης) ετη ιϐ'.

13. Acherrhes 12 years.

ιδ'. Αρμεσης (Αρμαις ὁ Δαναος) ετη ε'.

14 Armeses 5 years

ιε' Ραμμεσσης (Αμμεσης ὁ και Αιγυπτος) ετως ἑν.

15 Rammesses 1 year.

ιϛ' Αμενωφ (Μενωφις) ετη ιθ'.

16. Amenoph 19 years.

Ομοι ετη σξγ'

Altogether 263 years.

THE NINETEENTH DYNASTY.

Εννεακαιδεκατη δυναστεια βασιλεων ζ'. Διοσπολιτων.

Of seven Diospolite kings.

α'. Σεθως ετη να'.

1. Sethos reigned 51 years

β'. Ραψακης (ραψης) ετη ξα'.

2. Rapsaces 61 years.

γ'. Αμμενεφθης (Αμενωφθις) ετη κ'.

3. Ammenephthes 20 years.

δ'. Ραμεσης ετη ξ'.

4. Rameses 60 years.

ε'. Αμμενεμνης (Αμμενεμμης) ετη ε'.

5 Ammenemnes 5 years.

ϛ'. Θουωρις, ὁ παρ' Ὁμηρῳ καλουμενος Πολυϐους ϛ'.

6 Thuoris, who is called by Homer Polybus

ζ΄ Αλκανδρος εφ' ου το Ιλιον
εαλω ετη ζ΄.

Ομου ετη σθ΄.

Ετι του αυτου δευτερου τομ-
ου, βασιλεις ϛ΄. ετη ,βρκα΄

7. Alcandrus 7 yeais, in whose time Ilion was taken

Altogether 209 years.

In this second book of Manetho are contained 96 kings and 2121 years.—*Syncel. Chron* 59 *to* 75.— *Euseb Chron*. 15 *to* 17.

THE THIRD BOOK OF MANETHO:

THE TWENTIETH DYNASTY.

ΕΙΚΟΣΤΗ δυναστεια βασι-
λεων Διοσπολιταν ιϐ'. οἱ εϐασιλευσαν ετη ρλε'.

Of 12 Diospolite kings, who reigned 135 years.

THE TWENTY-FIRST DYNASTY.

Πρωτη και εικοστη δυνασ-
τεια βασιλεων Τανιτων ζ'

Of seven Tanite kings.

α'. Σμεδης (Σμελδης) ετη
λϛ'

1 Smedes reigned 26 years.

β'. Ψουσενης, η Ψαινεσης
(Ψουσεννης) ετη μϛ'.

2. Psusenes, or Psuneses, 46 years.

γ'. Νεφελχερης (Νεφερχε-
νης) ετη δ'.

3. Nephelcheres 4 years.

δ'. Αμενενωφθις (Αμενωφ-
θις) ετη θ'.

4. Amenophthis 9 years.

ε' Οσοχορ(Οσοχωρ)ετη ϛ'.

5. Osochor 6 years.

ϛ' Πιναχης (Ψιναχης) ετη
θ'.

6. Pinaches 9 years.

ζ'. Σουσεννης (Ψουσεννης)
ετη λ'.

7. Susenes 30 years

Ομου ετη ρλ'.

Altogether 130 years.

THE TWENTY-SECOND DYNASTY

Ειϲοϲτη δευτερα δυναϲτεια Βουβαϲτιτων βαϲιλεων θ'.

Of nine Bubastite kings.

Πρωτοϲ Σεϲογχιϲ (Σεϲεγ-χωϲιϲ) ετη κα'.

1. Sesonchis 21 years

β'. Οϲωρωθ (Οϲορθων) ετη ιε'

2. Osoroth 15 years.

γ' δ'. ε'. Αλλοι τρειϲ ετη νε'.

3, 4, 5 Three others reigned 25 years

ϛ'. Τακελλωθιϲ ετη ιγ'.

6 Tacelloths 13 years

ζ' η' θ'. Αλλοι τρειϲ ετη με'.

7, 8, 9. Three others 42 years

Ομου ετη ρκ'.

Altogether reigned 120 years

THE TWENTY-THIRD DYNASTY

ΚΓ'. δυναϲτεια Τανιτων βαϲιλεων δ'.

Of four Tanite kings.

α'. Πετουβατηϲ (Πετου-βαϲτηϲ) ετη μ'. εφ' ου Ολυμ-πιαϲ ηχθη πρωτη

1 Petoubates reigned 40 years, in whose time the Olympiads began

β'. Οϲορχω (Οϲορθων) ετη η'. ον 'Ηρακλεα Αιγυπτ.οι καλουϲιν.

2 Osorcho 8 years, whom the Egyptians call Hercules.

γ'. Ψαμμουϲ ετη ι'.

3. Psammus 10 years.

δ'. Ζητ ετη λα'.

4. Zeet 31 years

Ομου ετη πθ'

Altogether 89 years

THE TWENTY-FOURTH DYNASTY.

ΚΔ'. δυναϲτεια.

Βοχχωριϲ (Βοκχωριϲ) Σαιτηϲ

Bonchoris the Saite reigned 6

ετη ϛ'. εφ' ού αρνιον εφθεγξατο   years, in whose reign a sheep spoke.
ετη ⲙϼ '.   990 years.

THE TWENTY-FIFTH DYNASTY

ΚΕ'. δυναστεια Αιθιοπων
βασιλεων τριων.

    Of three Ethiop kings.

α'. Σαββακων, ὁς αιχμα-
λωτον Βοχχωριν ἑλων εκαυσε
ζωντα, και εβασιλευσεν ετη η'

    1. Sabbacon, who having taken Bonchoris a captive, burnt him alive, and reigned 8 years

β'. Σευηχος υίος ετη ιδ'.

    2. Seuechus, his son, reigned 14 years.

γ' Ταοκος (Ταρακος) ετη
ιη'.

    3 Tarcus 18 years

Ομου ετη μ'.

    Altogether 40 years.

THE TWENTY-SIXTH DYNASTY.

'Εκτη και εικοστη δυνασ-
τεια Σαιτα βασιλεων εννεα

    Of nine Saite kings

α' Στεφινατης (Στεφανα-
θις) ετη ζ'.

    1. Stephinates reigned 7 years.

β'. Νερεψως (Νεχεψως)
ετη ϛ'.

    2 Nerepsos 6 years

γ'. Νεχαω ετη η'

    3. Nechao 8 years.

δ'. Ψαμμιτικος (Ψαμμιτι-
χος,) ετη νδ'.

    4. Psammiticus 54 years.

ε' Νεχαω δευτερος ετη ϛ'.
ούτος είλε την 'Ιερουσαλημ,
και Ιωαχας τον βασιλεα εις
Αιγυπτον απηγαγεν.

    5. Nechao the second 6 years. He took Jerusalem, and carried Joachas, the king, to Egypt.

ϛ'. Ψαμμουθις ἑτερος ετη
ξζ'

    6. Psammuthius 6 years.

ζ'. Ουαφρις (Ουαφρης) ετη
ιθ'. ᾧ προσεφυγον ἁλουσης ὑπο

    7. Vaphris 19 years, to whom the remainder of the Jews fled when

Ασσυριων Ἱερουσαλημ οἱ των   Jerusalem was taken by the Assy-
Ἰουδαιων ὑπολοιποι.   rians

η'. Αμασις ετη μδ'.   8 Amosis 44 years

θ'. Ψαμμαχεριτης* μηνας   9. Psammacherites 6 months.
ς'.

Ὁμου ετη ρν'. και μηνας ς'.   Altogether 150 years and six
                                  months

THE TWENTY-SEVENTH DYNASTY.

ΚΖ'. βασιλεια Περσων βα-   Of eight Persian kings
σιλεων η'.

α' Καμβυσης ετη ε' ~ης   1. Cambyses reigned over Persia,
ἑαυτου βασιλειας.   Περσων   his own kingdom, 5 years, and over
εβασιλευσεν Αιγυπτου ετη ς'   Egypt 6 years.

β'. Δαρειος Ὑστασπου ετη   2. Darius, the son of Hystaspes,
λς'.   36 years

γ Ξερξης ὁ μεγας ετη να'   3. Xerxes the Great 21 years.

δ' Αρταβανος † μηνας ζ'.   4. Artabanus 7 months.

ε' Αρταξερξης ετη μα'.   5. Artaxerxes 41 years.

ς'. Ξερξης μηνας δυο.   6 Xerxes 2 months.

ζ' Σογδιανος μηνας ζ'.   7. Sogdianus 7 months.

η' Δαρειος Ξερξου ιθ'.   8. Darius the son of Xerxes, 19
                                  years.

Ὁμου ετη ρκδ'. μηνας δ'.   Altogether 124 years and four
                                  months.

---

* Eusebius omits the last, and inserts Αμμιρης at the beginning as the first
† Eusebius omits Artabanus, and between Cambyses and Darius places the
Magi, with a reign of seven months

THE TWENTY-EIGHTH DYNASTY

ΚΗ'. δυναστεια.

Αμιρτεως (Αμυρταιος) Σαι-
της ετη ϛ'.

Amyrteos, the Saite, 6 years.

THE TWENTY-NINTH DYNASTY

ΚΘ'. δυναστε.α Μενδησιων
βασιλεων δ'.

Of four Mendesian kings.

α'. Νεφερειτης (Νεφεριτης)
ετη ϛ'.

1. Nepherites reigned 6 years

β'. Αχωρις ετη ιγ'.

2. Achoris 13 years.

γ'. Ψαμμουθις ετος α'

3. Psammuthis 1 year.

δ'. Νεφοροτης (Αναφεριτης
Νεφεριτης) μηνας δ'.

4 Nephorotes 4 months.

(ε'. Μουθις ετος α'.)

(5 Muthis 1 year)

Ομου ετη ν'. μηνας δ'.

Altogether 20 years and four
months.

THE THIRTIETH DYNASTY.

Τριακοστη δυναστεια Σε-
βεννυταν βασιλεων τριων

Of three Sebennyte kings.

α'. Νεκτανεβης (Νεκτανε-
βις) ετη ιη'

1. Nectanebes 18 years.

β' Τεως ετη β'.

2 Teos 2 years

γ'. Νεκτανεβης (Νεκτανε-
βος) ετη ιη'.

3. Nectanebes 18 years.

Ομου ετη λη'.

Altogether 38 years.

THE THIRTY-FIRST DYNASTY

ΛΑ'. δυναστεια Περταν
βασιλεων τριων.

Of three Persian kings.

α΄. Ὦχος εικοστῳ ετει της ἑαυτου βασιλειας Περσων εβασιλευσεν Αιγυπτου ετη β΄.

1. Ochus ruled Persia twenty years, and Egypt 2 years.

β΄. Αρσης (Αρσης Ωχου) ετη γ΄.

2. Arses reigned 3 years.

γ΄. Δαρειος ετη δ΄.
Ομου ετη θ΄.
Ομου ͵αν΄.

3. Darius 4 years.
Altogether 9 years.
And the whole 1050 years.—
Syncel. Chron. 73 *to* 78. — *Euseb. Chron.* 16, 17.

MANETHO:

OF THE SHEPHERD KINGS

ΕΓΕΝΕΤΟ βασιλευς ἡμιν, Τιμαιος ονομα, επι τουτου ουκ οιδ᾽ ὁπως ὁ Θεος αντεπνευσεν, και παραδοξως εκ των προς αρατολην μερων, ανθρωποι το γενος ασημοι, καταθαρσησαντες επι την χωραν εστρατευσαν, και ῥαδιως αμαχητι ταυτην κατα κρατος εἱλον και τους ἡγεμονευσαντας εν αυτη χειρωσαμενοι, το λοιπον τας τε πολεις ωμως ενεπρησαν, και τα ἱερα των Θεων κατεσκαψαν πασι δε τοις επιχωριοις εχθροτατα πως εχρησαντο, τους μεν σφαζοντες, των δε και τα τεκνα και γυναικας εις δουλειαν αγοντες περας δε και βασιλεα ἑνα εξ αυτων εποιησαν, ᾧ ονομα ην Σαλατις και οὑτος εν τη Μεμφιδι κατεγινετο, την τε ανω και κατω χωραν δασμολογων, και φρουραν εν τοις επιτηδειοτατοις

We had formerly a king whose name was Timaus. In his time it came to pass, I know not how, that God was displeased with us and there came up from the East in a strange manner men of an ignoble race, who had the confidence to invade our country, and easily subdued it by their power without a battle And when they had our rulers in their hands, they burnt our cities, and demolished the temples of the gods, and inflicted every kind of barbarity upon the inhabitants, slaying some, and reducing the wives and children of others to a state of slavery. At length they made one of themselves king, whose name was Salatis : he lived at Memphis, and rendered both the upper and lower regions of Egypt tributary, and stationed garrisons in places which were best adapted for that purpose. But he directed his attention principally to the security

καταλειπων τοποις μαλιστα
δε και τα προς ανατολην ησ-
φαλισατο μερη, προορωμενος
Ασσυριων, τοτε μειζον ισχυον-
των, εσομενην επιθυμιαν της
αυτης βασιλειας εφοδου εἰρων
δε εν νομω τω Σαιτη πολιν
επικαιροτατην, νειμενην μεν
προς ανατολην του Βουβαττι-
του ποταμου, καλουμενην δ'
απο τινος αρχαιας θεολογιας
Αναριν, ταυτην εκτισεν τε,
και τοις τειχεσιν οχυρωτατην
εποιησεν ενοικισας αυτη και
πληθος ὁπλιτων εις εικοσι και
τεσσαρας μιριαδας αλδρων προς
φυλακην ενθαδε κατα θερειαν
ηρχετο, τα μεν σιτομετρων και
μισθοφοριαν παρεχομενος, τα
δε και ται, εξοπλισιαις προς
φοβον των εξωθεν επιμελες
γυμναζων.

Αρξας δ' εννεακαιδεκα ετη
τον βιον ετελευτησαν Μετα
τουτον δε ἑτερος εβασιλευσεν
τεσσαρα και τετταρακοντα
ετη, καλουμενος Βηων. μεθ'
ὁν αλλος Απαχνας, ἑξ και τριακοντα ετη και μηνας ἑπτα.
επειτα δε και Απωφις ἑν και
ἑξηκοντα, και Ιανιας πεντηκοντα και μηνα ἑνα. επι πασι
δε και Ασσις εννεα και τεσσαρακοντα και μηνας δυο. Και
οὑτοι μεν ἑξ εν αιτοις εγενηθησαν πρωτοι αρχοντες, πολε-

of the eastern frontier ; for he regard-
ed with suspicion the increasing
power of the Assyrians, who he
foresaw would one day undertake an
invasion of the kingdom. And ob-
serving in the Saite nome, upon the
east of the Bubastite channel, a city
which from some ancient theological
reference was called Avaris, and
finding it admirably adapted to his
purpose, he rebuilt it, and strongly
fortified it with walls, and garrisoned
it with a force of two hundred and
fifty thousand armed men To this
city Salatis repaired in summer time,
to collect his tribute, and pay his
troops, and to exercise his soldiers
in order to strike terror into foreigners.

And Salatis died after a reign of
nineteen years . after him reigned Beon
forty-four years and he was succeeded
by Apachnas who reigned thirty-six
years and seven months after him
reigned Apophis sixty-one years, and
Ianias fifty years and one month. After
all these reigned Assis forty-nine years
and two months These six were the
first rulers amongst them, and during
all the period of their dynasty, they
made war upon the Egyptians in
hope of exterminating the whole
race. All this nation was styled

μοιυτες αει και ποθουντες μαλ-
λον της Αιγυπτου εξαραι την
ριζαν. Εκαλειτο δε το συμ-
παν αυτων εθνος Ὑκσως, τουτο
δε εστι βασιλεις ποιμενες. το
γαρ Ὑκ καθ᾽ ἱεραν γλωσσαν
βασιλεα σημαινει, το δε Σως
ποιμην εστι και ποιμενες κατα
την κοινην διαλεκτον, και ουτω
συντιθεμενον γινεται Ὑκσως.
τινες δε λεγουσιν αυτους Αρα-
βας ειναι. Τουτους δε τους
προκατανομασμενους βασιλεας
τοις των ποιμενων καλουμενων,
και τους εξ αυτων γενομενους,
κρατησαι της Αιγυπτου (φησιν)
ειη προς τοις πεντακοσιοις ενδεκα.

Μετα ταυτα δε, των εκ της
Θεβαιδος και της αλλης Αιγυπτου βασιλεων γενεσθαι (φησιν)
επι τους ποιμενας επαναστασιν,
και πολεμον αυτοις συρραγηναι
μεγαν και πολυχρονιον. επι δε
βασιλεως, ῳ ονομα ειναι Αλισ-
φραγμουθωσις, ητ]ωμενους (φησι) τους ποιμενας ὑπ᾽ αυτου,
εκ μεν της αλλης Αιγυπτου
πασης εκπεσειν, κατακλεισθη-
ναι δ᾽ εις τοπον, αρουρων εχοντα
μυριων την περιμετρον. Αυαριν
ονομα τῳ τοπῳ. Τουτον (φησιν
ὁ Μανεθων) ἁπαντα, τειχει
τε μεγαλῳ και ισχυρῳ περι-
βαλειν τους ποιμενας, ὁπως την
τε κτησιν ἁπασαν εχωσιν εν
οχυρῳ, και την λειαν την ἑαυ]ων.

Hycsos, that is the Shepherd Kings; for the first syllable, Hyc, according to the sacred dialect, denotes a king, and Sos signifies a shepherd, but this according to the vulgar tongue; and of these is compounded the term Hycsos: some say they were Arabians. This people, who were thus denominated Shepherd Kings, and their descendants retained possession of Egypt for the space of five hundred and eleven years.

After these things he relates that the kings of Thebaïs and of the other parts of Egypt, made an insurrection against the Shepherds, and that a long and mighty war was carried on between them, till the Shepherds were subdued by a king whose name was Alisphragmuthosis, and were by him driven out of the rest of Egypt, and hemmed within a place containing ten thousand acres, which was called Avaris. All this tract (says Manetho) the Shepherds surrounded with a vast and strong wall, that they might retain all their possessions and their prey within a hold of strength.

Τον δε Αλισφραγμουθωσεως
υἱον Θουμμωσιν επιχειρησαι
μεν αυτους δια πολιορκιας ἑλειν
κατα κρατος, οκτω και τεσσαρακοντα μυριασι προσεδρευ-
σαντα τοις τειχεσιν· επει δε
της πολιορκιας απεγνω, ποιη-
σασθαι συμβασεις, ἱνα την
Αιγυπτον εκλιποντες ὁτοι βου-
λονται παντες αβλαβεις απελ-
θωσι. τοις δε επι ταις ὁμολο-
γιαις πανοικεσιᾳ μετα των
κτησεων συν ελαττους μυριαδων
οντας εικοσι και τεσσαραν απο
της Αιγυπτου την ερημον εις
Συριαν ὁδοιπορησαι. φοβουμεν-
ους δε την Ασσυριων δυναστειαν,
τοτε γαρ εκεινους της Ασιας
κρατειν, εν τη νυν Ιουδαιᾳ
καλουμενη πολιν οικοδομησα-
μενους τοσαυταις μυριασιν
ανθρωπων αρκεσουσαν, Ἱεροσολυμα ταυτην ονομασαι.

(Εν αλλη δε τινι βιβλῳ των
Αιγυπτιακων Μανεθων) Τουτο
(φησιν) εθνος τους καλουμενους
ποιμενας, αιχμαλωτους εν ταις
ἱεραις αυτων βιβλοις γεγραφθαι.

Μετα το εξελθειν εξ Αιγυπτου τον λαον των ποιμενων εις
Ἱεροσολυμα, ὁ εκβαλων αυτους
εξ Αιγυπτου βασιλευς Τεθμω-
σις, εβασιλευσεν μετα ταυτα
ετη εικοσι πεντε και μηνας
τεσσαρας, και ετελευτησεν,
και παρελαβε την αρχην αυτου

And Thummosis, the son of Alisphragmuthosis, endeavoured to force
them by a siege, and beleaguered the
place with a body of four hundred
and eighty thousand men; but at
the moment when he despaired of
reducing them by siege, they agreed
to a capitulation, that they would
leave Egypt, and should be permitted
to go out without molestation where-
soever they pleased. And, according
to this stipulation, they departed from
Egypt with all their families and
effects, in number not less than two
hundred and forty thousand, and bent
their way through the desert towards
Syria. But as they stood in fear of
the Assyrians, who had then dominion over Asia, they built a city in
that country which is now called
Judæa, of sufficient size to contain
this multitude of men, and named it
Jerusalem

(In another book of the Egyptian
histories Manetho says) That this
people, who are here called Shepherds, in their sacred books were also
styled Captives

After the departure of this nation
of Shepherds to Jerusalem, Tethmosis, the king of Egypt who drove
them out, reigned twenty-five years
and four months, and then died·
after him his son Chebron took the
government into his hands for thirteen years, after him reigned Ameno-

υἱὸς Χεβρων ετη δεκατρια μεθ'
ὃν Ἀμεναφις εινοσι ϰαι μηνας
ἑπτα. του δε αδελφη Αμεσσης
εικοσι ἑν και μηνα, εινεα. της
δε Μηφρης δωδεκα και μηνας
εννεα. του δε Μηφραμουθωσις
εικοσι πεντε και μηνας δεκα.
του δε Θμωσι, εννεα ϰαι μηνας
οϰτω του δε Αμεναφις τριακοντα και μηνας δεϰα του δε
Ωρος τριακοντα ἑξ και μηνας
πεντε του δε Θυγατηρ Ακεγ-
χρης δωδεκα και μηνα ἑνα
της δε Ραθωτις αδελφος εννεα
του δε Ακεγχηρης δωδεκα ϰαι
μηνας πεντε. του δε Αϰεγ-
χηρης ἑτερος δωδεϰα και μηνας
τρεις του δε Αρμαις τεσσαρα
ϰαι μηνα ἑνα του δε Ραμεσσης ἑν και μηνας τεσσαρας
του δε Αρμεσσης Μιαμμου εξη-
ϰοντα ἑξ και μηνας δυο του
δε Αμελωφις δεϰα ϰαι εννεα
ϰαι μηνας ἑξ. του δε Σεθωσις,
ϰαι Ραμεσσης, ἱππικην και
ναυτικην εχων δυναμιν

Οὗτος τον μεν αδελφον
Αρμαιν επιτροπον της Αιγυπτου
ϰατεστησεν, και πασαν μεν
αυτω την αλλην βασιλικην
περιεθηϰεν εξουσιαν, μονον δε
ενετειλατο διαδημα μη φορειν,
μηδε την βασιλιδα μητερα τε
των τεκνων αδιϰειν, απεχεσθαι
δε και των αλλων βασιλικων
παλλακιδων. αυτος δε επι

phis for twenty years and seven
months then his sister Amesses
twenty-one years and nine months:
she was succeeded by Mephres, who
reigned twelve years and nine months ·
after him Mephramuthosis twenty-
five years and ten months: then
Thmosis reigned nine years and eight
months, after whom Amenophis
thirty years and ten months then
Orus thirty-six years and five months:
then his daughter Acencbres twelve
years and one month · after her
Rathotis nine years. then Acencheres twelve years and five months.
another Acencheres twelve years and
three months after him Armais four
years and one month after him reigned
Ramesses one year and four months.
then Armesses the son of Miammous
sixty-six years and two months after
him Amenophis nineteen years and
six months: and he was succeeded by
Sethosis who is called Ramesses, he
maintained an army of cavalry and a
naval force.

This king (Sethosis) appointed his
brother Armais his viceroy over
Egypt: he also invested him with all
the other authority of a king, but with
these restrictions; that he should not
wear the diadem, nor interfere with
the queen, the mother of his children,
nor abuse the royal concubines. Sethosis then made an expedition against
Cyprus and Phœnicia, and waged

Κιτρον και Φοινικην και παλιν
Ασσυριους τε και Μηδους ςρα-
τευσας, άπαντας, τους μεν
δορατι, τους δε αμαχητι, φοβῳ
δε της πολλης δυναμεως, ύπο-
χειρ.ους ελαβε. και μεγα
φρονησας επι ταις ευπραγιαις,
ετι και ϑαρσαλεωτερον επο-
ρευετο, τας προς αυατολας
πολεις τε και χωρας κατα-
στρεφομενος

Χρονου τε ίκανου γεγονοτος,
Αρμαις ό καταλειφθεις εν Αι-
γυπτῳ, παντα τοιμπαλιν, οίς
αδελφος παρηνει μη ποιειν,
αδεως επραττεν και γαρ την
βασιλιδα βιαιως εσχεν, ναι
ταις αλλαις παλλανισιν αφει-
δας διετελει χρωμενος. πειθο-
μενος δε ύπο των φιλων διαδημα
εφορει. και αντηρε τῳ αδελφῳ.

Ό δε τεταγμενος επι των
ίερων της Αιγυπτου, γραψας
βιβλιον επεμψε τῳ Σεθωσει,
δηλων αυτῳ παντα, και ότι
αντηρεν ό αδελφος αυτου Αρ·
μαις. παραχρημα ουν ύπε-
στρεψεν εις Πηλουσιον, και
εκρατησεν της ιδιας βασιλειας
ή δε χωρα εκληθη απο του αυτου
ονοματος Αιγυπτος. λεγει γαρ
ότι ό μεν Σεθωσις εναλειτο
Αιγυπτος, Αρμαις δε ό Αδελφος αυτου Δαναος.

war with the Assyrians and Medes ,
and he subdued them all, some by
force of arms, and others without a
blow, by the mere terror of his power.
And being puffed up with his success,
he advanced still more confidently,
and overthrew the cities, and subdued
the countries of the East.

But Armais, who was left in Egypt,
took advantage of the opportunity,
and fearlessly committed all those acts
which his brother had enjoined him
not to do. he violated the queen, and
continued an unrestrained intercourse
with the rest, and at the persuasion
of his friends he assumed the diadem,
and openly opposed his brother

But the ruler over the priests of
Egypt sent to Sethosis, and informed
him of what had happened, and how
his brother had set himself up in
opposition to his power. Upon this
Sethosis immediately returned to Pe-
lusium, and recovered his kingdom.
The country of Egypt took its name
from Sethosis, who was called also
Ægyptus, as was his brother Armais
known by the name of Danaus.—
Joseph. contr. App. lib I. c. 14, 15.

L

OF THE ISRAELITES

Τουτον (Αμενωφιν) επιθυμη-
σαι θεων γενεσθαι θεατην,
ὡσπερ Ωρος εἰς των προ αυτου
βεβασιλευκοτων· ανενεγκειν δε
την επιθυμιαν ὁμωνυμῳ μεν
αιτῳ Αμενωφει, πατρος δε
Παπιος οντι, θειας δε δοκουντι
μετεσχηκεναι φυσεως, κατα
τε σοφιαν και προγνωσιν των
εσομενων. ειπειν ουν αυτῳ
τουτον τον ὁμωνυμον, ὁτι δυνη-
σεται θεοις ιδειν, ει καθαραν
απο τε λεπρων και των αλλων
μιαρων ανθρωπων την χωραν
ἁπασαν ποιησειεν.

'Ησθεντα δε τον βασιλεα,
παντας τους τα σωματα λελω-
βημενους εκ της Αιγυπτου συν-
αγαγειν· γενεσθαι δε του πλη-
θους μυριαδας οκτω· και τουτους
εις τας λιθοτομιας τας εν τῳ
προς ανατολην μερει του Νειλου
εμβαλειν αυτον, ὁπως εργα-
ζοιντο και των αλλων Αιγυπτιων
οἱ εγκεχωρισμενοι. ειναι δε
τινας εν αυτοις και των λογιων
ἱερεων (φησι,) λεπρᾳ συγκεχυ-
μενους. τον δε Αμενωφιν εκει-
νον, τον σοφον και μαντινον
ανδρα, ὑποδεισθαι προς αυτον
τε και τον βασιλεα χολον των
θεων, ει βιασθεντες οφθησον-

This king (Amenophis) was desirous of beholding the gods, as Orus, one of his predecessors in the kingdom, had seen them   And he communicated his desire to a priest of the same name with himself, Amenophis, the son of Papis, who seemed to partake of the divine nature, both in his wisdom and knowledge of futurity   and Amenophis returned him answer, that he might behold the gods, if he would cleanse the country of all lepers and other unclean persons that were in it

Well pleased with this information, the king gathered together out of the land of Egypt all that laboured under any defect in body, to the amount of eighty thousand, and sent them to the quarries, which are situate on the east side of the Nile, that they might work in them and be separated from the rest of the Egyptians   And (he says) there were among them some learned priests who were affected with leprosy.   And Amenophis the wise man and prophet, fearful lest the vengeance of the gods should fall both on himself and on the king, if it should appear that violence had been offered them, added this also

ται. και προσθεμενον ειπειν,
ότι συμμαχησουσι τινες τοις
μιαροις, και της Αιγυπτου
κρατησουσιν επ' ετη δεκατρια.
μη τολμησαι μεν αυτον ειπειν
ταυτα τῳ βασιλει, γραφην δε
καταλιποντα περι παντων ἑαυτον ανελειν. εν αθυμια δε ειναι
τον βασιλεα

(Κατειτα κατα λεξιν οίτω
γεγοαφεν). Των δε ταις λατο-
μιαις ἁς χρονος ἱκανος διηλθεν
ταλαιπωρουντων, αξιωθεις ὁ
βασιλευς, ἱνα προς καταλυσιν
αυτοις και σκεπην απομεριση
την τοτε των ποιμενων ερημω-
θεισαν πολιν, Αυαριν συνεχω-
ρησεν. εστι δε ἡ πολις κατα
την θεολογιαν ανωθεν Τυφωνιος.

Οἱ δε εις ταυτην εισελ-
θοντες, και τον τοπον τουτον
εις αποςασιν εχοντες, ἡγεμονα
αὑτων λεγομενον τινα των
'Ηλιοπολιτων ἱερων Οσαρσιφον
εστησαντο. και τουτω πειθαρ-
χησοντες εν πασιν ὡρκομοτη-
σαν ὁ δε πρωτον μεν αυτοις
νομον εθετο, μητε προσκυνειν
θεοις, μητε των μαλιστα εν
Αιγυπτω θεμιστευομενων ἱερων
ζωων απεχεσθαι μηδενος, παντα τε θυειν και αναλουν·
συναπτεσθαι δε μηδενι πλην
των συνωμοσμενων. τοιαντα δε

in a prophetic spirit;—that certain people would come to the assistance of these polluted wretches, and would subdue Egypt, and hold it in possession for thirteen years. These tidings however he dared not to communicate to the king, but left in writing an account of what should come to pass, and destroyed himself, at which the king was fearfully distressed.

(After which he writes thus, word for word·) When those that were sent to work in the quarries had continued for some time in that miserable state, the king was petitioned to set apart for their habitation and protection the city Avaris, which had been left desolate by the Shepherds, and he granted them their desire: now this city, according to the theology above, is a Typhonian city.

When these men had taken possession of the city, and found it well adapted for a revolt, they appointed over themselves a ruler out of the priests of Heliopolis, one whose name was Osarsiph, and they bound themselves by oath that they would be obedient. Osarsiph then, in the first place enacted this law, that they should neither worship the gods, nor abstain from any of those sacred animals which the Egyptians hold in the highest veneration, but sacrifice and slay them all, and that they should connect themselves with none but

νομοθετησας, και πλειστα
αλλα, μαλιστα τοις Αιγυπ-
τιοις εθισμοις εναντιουμενα,
εκελευσεν πολυχειρια τα της
πολεως επισκευαζειν τειχη, και
προς πολεμον έτοιμους γινεσθαι
τον προς Αμενωφιν τον βασιλεα. αυτος δε προσλαβομενος
μεθ' έαυτου και των αλλων
ίερεων και συμμεμιασμενων,
επεμψε πρεσβεις προς τους ύπο
Τεθμωσεως απελαθεντας ποιμενας, εις πολιν την ναλουμενην
'Ιεροσολιμα και τα καθ' έαυτον και τους αλλους τους συν-
ατιμασθεντας δηλωσας, ηξιου
συνεπιστρατευειν ὁμοθυμαδον
επ' Αιγυπτον. επαξειν μεν ουν
αυτους επηγγειλατο, πρωτον
μεν εις Αυαριν την προγονικην
αυτων πατριδα, και τα επιτη-
δεια τοις οχλοις παρεξειν αφ-
θονως, ὑπερμαχησεσθαι δε οτε
δεοι, και ῥᾳδιως ὑποχειριον
αυτοις την χωραν ποιησειν. οἱ
δε ὑπερχαρεις γενομενοι παντες
προθυμως εις εινοσι μυριαδας
ανδρων σινεξωρμησαν, και μετ'
ου πολι ήνον εις Αυαριν.

Αμενωφις δ' ὁ των Αιγυπ-
τιων βασιλευς, ὡς επιθετο τα
κατα την εκεινων εφοδον, ου

such as were of that confederacy.
When he had made such laws as
these, and many others of a tendency
directly in opposition to the customs
of the Egyptians, he gave orders that
they should employ the multitude of
hands in rebuilding the walls about
the city, and hold themselves in
readiness for war with Amenophis
the king, whilst he took into his
confidence and counsels some others
of the priests and unclean persons:
and he sent ambassadors to the city
called Jerusalem, to those Shepherds
who had been expelled by Tethmosis,
whereby he informed them of the
affairs of himself and of the others
who had been treated in the same
ignominious manner, and requested
they would come with one consent to
his assistance in this war against
Egypt. He also promised in the first
place to reinstate them in their ancient
city and country Avaris, and provide
a plentiful maintenance for their host,
and fight for them as occasion might
require, and informed them that they
could easily reduce the country under
dominion. The Shepherds received
this message with the greatest joy,
and quickly mustered to the number
of two hundred thousand men, and
came up to Avaris.

Now Amenophis the king of Egypt,
when he was informed of their invasion, was in great consternation,

μετρίως συνεχύθη, της παρ'
Αμεναφεως του Παπιος μνησ-
θεις προδηλωσεως. και προτερον
συναγαγων πληθος Αιγυπτιων,
και βουλευσαμενος μετα των
εν τουτοις ηγεμονων, τα τε ιερα
ζωα τα πρωτα μαλιστα εν
τοις ιεροις τιμωμενα ώς γ' έαυτον μετεπεμψατο, και τοις
κατα μερος ιερευσιν παρηγγει-
λεν, ώς ασφαλεστατα των
θεων συγκρυψαι τα ξοανα
τον δε υίον Σεθων τον και
Ραμεσσην απο Ραμψεως του
πατρος ωνομασμενον πεντα-
ετη οντα, εξεθετο προς τον
έαυτου φιλον. αυτος δε διαβας
τοις αλλοις Αιγυπτιοις, ουσιν
εις τριακοντα μυριαδας ανδρων
μαχιμωτατων, και τοις πολε-
μιοις απαντησασιν ου συνεβα-
λεν αλλα μελλειν θεομαχειν
νομισας, παλινδρομησας ήκεν
εις Μεμφιν. αναλαβων τε τον
τε Απιν, και τα αλλα τα
εκεισε μεταπεμφθεντα ιερα
ζωα, ευθυς εις Αιθιοπιαν συν
άπαντι τω στολω και πληθει
των Αιγυπτιων ανηχθη. χαριτι
γαρ ην αυτα υποχειριος ό των
Αιθιοπων βασιλευς· όθεν υπο-
δεξαμενος, και τους οχλους
παντας υπολαβων οίς εσχεν ή
χωρα των προς ανθρωπινην
τροφην επιτηδειαν, και πολεις
και κωμας προς την των πε-

remembering the prophecy of Amenophis, the son of Papis, and he assembled the armies of the Egyptians, and
took counsel with the leaders, and
commanded the sacred animals to be
brought to him, especially those which
were held in the greatest veneration in
the temples, and particularly charged
the priests to conceal the images of
their gods with the utmost care And
his son Sethos, who was also called
Ramesses from his father Rampses,
being but five years old he committed to the protection of a friend.
And he marched with the rest of the
Egyptians being three hundred thousand warriors, against the enemy, who
advanced to meet him, but he did
not attack them, thinking it would be
to wage war against the gods, but he
returned, and came again to Memphis, where he took Apis and the other
sacred animals he had sent for, and
retreated immediately into Ethiopia
together with all his army, and all the
multitude of the Egyptians: for the
king of Ethiopia was under obliga-
tions to him, wherefore he received
him kindly, and took care of all the
multitude that was with him, while
the country supplied all that was
necessary for their food. He also
allotted to him cities and villages
during his exile, which was to continue from its beginning during the
predestined thirteen years. More-

πρωμενον τρισκαιδεκα ετων απο
της αρχης αυτου εκπτωσιν
αυταρκεις, ουκ ήττον γε και
στρατοπεδον Αιθιοπικον προς
φυλακην επεταξε τοις παρ'
Αμενωφεως του βασιλεως επι
των δριων της Αιγυπτου.

Και τα μεν κατα την
Αιθιοπιαν τοιαυτα. οἱ δε Σολυ-
μιται κατελθοντες, συν τοις
μιαροις των Αιγυπτιων οὑτως
ανοσιως τοις ανθρωποις προσ-
ηνηχθησαν, ὡστε την των
προειρημενον κρατησιν χειρισ-
την φαινεσθαι, τοις τοτε τα
τουτων ασεβηματα θεωμενοις.
και γαρ ου μονον πολεις και
κωμας ενεπρησαν, ουδε ἱερο-
σολουντες, ουδε λυμαινομενοι
ξοανα θεων ηρκουντο, αλλα
και τοις αυτοις οπτανιοις των
σεβαστευομενων ἱερων ζωων
χραμενοι διετελουν, και θοτας
ναι σφαγεις τουτων ἱερεις και
πρφητας ηναγκαζον γινεσθαι,
ναι γυμνους εξεβαλον. λεγεται
δ' ὁτι την πολιτειαν και τους
νομους αυτοις καταβαλλομενος
ἱερευς, το γενος Ἡλιουπολιτης,
ονομα Οσαρσιφ, απο του εν
Ἡλιου πολει θεου Οσιρεως, ὡς
μετεβη εις τουτο το γενος,
μετετεθη τουνομα και προσ-
γορειθη Μωισης.

over he pitched a camp for an Ethio-
pian army upon the borders of Egypt,
as a protection to king Amenophis

While such was the state of things
in Ethiopia, the people of Jerusalem,
having come down with the unclean
of the Egyptians, treated the inhabitants with such barbarity, that those
who witnessed their impieties believed
that their joint sway was more exe-
crable than that which the Shepherds
had formerly exercised for they not
only set fire to the cities and villages,
but committed every kind of sacrilege,
and destroyed the images of the gods,
and roasted and fed upon those sacred
animals that were worshipped, and
having compelled the priests and
prophets to kill and sacrifice them,
they cast them naked out of the
country It is said also that the priest,
who ordained their polity and laws, was
by birth of Heliopolis, and his name
Osarsiph, from Osiris the god of Heliopolis: but that when he went over
to these people his name was changed,
and he was called Moyses.—*Joseph.
contr App.* lib. I c. 26.

ΟΓ THE ISRAELITES

(Λεγει δε ὁ Μανεθων παλιν.)
τι μετα ταυτα επηλθεν ὁ
λενωφις απο Αιθιοπιας μετα
γαλης δυναμεως, και ὁ υίος
'του Ραμψης και αυτος εχων
ναμιν· και συμβαλοντες οἱ δυο
ις ποιμεσι και τοις μιαροις,
κησαν αυτους, και πολλους
τοκτειναντες εδιαξαν αυτους
ζρι των ὁριων της Συριας.

(Manetho again says) After this Amenophis returned from Ethiopia with a great force, and Rampses also, his son, with other forces, and encountering the Shepherds and the unclean people, they defeated them and slew multitudes of them, and pursued them to the bounds of Syria. — *Joseph. contr App* lib I. c 27

ERATOSTHENES'

ΠΡΩΤΟΣ εβασιλευσεν Μινης Θηβινιτης Θηβαιος, ὁ ἑρμηνευεται Διονιος· εβασιλευσεν ετη ξβ'. του δε κοσμου ην ετος ,βπ'

Θηβαιαν δευτερος εβασιλευσεν Αθωθης υιος Μινεως ετη νθ'. ουτος ἑρμηνευεται Ἑρμογενης ετος του κοσμου, ,βϡξβ'

Θηβαιων Αιγυπτιων τριτος εβασιλευσεν Αθωθης ὁμωνυμος ετη λβ' του δε κοσμου ην ετος, ,γκα'.

Θηβαιων εβασιλευσεν δ'. Διαβιης υιος Αθωσεως ετη ιθ'. ουτος ἑρμηνευεται Φιλεστερος· του δε κοσμου ην ετος, ,γνγ'.

Θηβαιων εβασιλευσεν ε'. Πεμφως υιος Αθωθου ὁ εστιν Ἡρακλειδης ετη ιη' του δε κοσμου ην ετος ,γοβ'.

Θηβαιων Αιγυπτιων εβασιλευσεν ϛ'. Τοιγαρ Αμαχος

THE first who reigned was Mines the Thebinite, the Thebæan; which is by interpretation Dionius. He reigned sixty-two years, and lived in the year of the world 2900.

The 2nd of the Theban kings reigned Athothes the son of Mines, 59 years. He is called by interpretation Hermogenes. In the year of the world 2962.

The 3rd of the Theban Egyptian kings was Athothes, of the same name, 32 years. In the year of the world 3021.

The 4th of the Theban kings was Diabies the son of Athothes, 19 years. By interpretation he is called Philesteros. In the year of the world 3053.

The 5th of the Theban kings was Pemphos, the son of Athothes, who is called Heraclides. He reigned 18 years. In the year of the world 3072.

The 6th of the Theban Egyptian kings was Tœgai Amachus Mom-

Ἰομχειρι Μεμφιτης ετη οθ' Ἰτος ἑρμηνευεται τις ανδρος ερισσομελης· του δε κοσμοι ην τος ‚γή'.

Θηβαιων Λιγυπτιων εβασιευσεν ζ'. Στοιχος ὁ υἱος αυτου, εστιν Αρης αναισθητος, ετη ' του δε κοσμου ην ετος, ‚ηρξθ'.

Θηβαιων Λιγυπτιων εβασιευσεν ογδοος Γοσορμιης, ὁ ττιν Ετησιπαντος ετη λ' τοι ε ‚κοσμου ην ε‑ος ‚γροε'.

Θηβαιων Λιγυπτιων εβασιευσεν θ'. Μαρης υἱος αυτου, εστιν Ἡλιοδωρος ετη λς'. ου κοσμου ην ετος γσε'.

Θηβαιων Λιγυπτιων ι'. εβαιλευσεν Ανωυφης, ὁ εστιν ἱος επινοινος ετη κ'. του κοσ‑ου ην ετος, ‚γσλα'.

Θηβαιων Λιγυπτιων ια'. βασιλευσεν Σιριος, ὁ εστιν ορρης, ὡς δε ἑτεροι Αβασκαν‑ος ετη ιη' του δε κοσμου ην τος, ‚γσ‑α'.

Θηβαιων Λιγυπτιων ιβ'‥ βασιλευσει Χνουβος Γνευρος, εστιν Χρυσης Χρυσου υἱος ‑η κβ'. του δε κοσμου ην ετος, γσξθ'.

Θηβαιων Λιγυπτιων ιγ'. βασιλευσεν Ρανωσις, ὁ εστιν εχρικραταρ ετη ιγ'. του δε ‑ασμου ην ετος, ‚γσ‑α'.

Θηβαιων Λιγυπτιων ιδ'.

chiri, the Memphite, who is called a man redundant in his members, 79 years and A. M. 3090.

The 7th of the Theban Egyptian kings, Stœchus his son, who is Ares the senseless, reigned 6 years. A. M 3169.

The 8th of the Theban Egyptian kings Gosormies, who is called Etesipantus, reigned 30 years, and A M. 3175.

The 9th of the Theban Egyptian kings Mares, his son, who is called Heliodorus, 26 years, and A. M. 3205.

The 10th of the Theban Egyptian kings Anoÿphes, which signifies a common son, reigned 20 years, and A. M 3231.

The 11th of the Theban Egyptian kings Sirius, which signifies the son of the cheek, but according to others Abascantus reigned 18 years, and A M 3251

The 12th of the Theban Egyptian kings reigned Chnubus Gneurus, which is Chryses the son of Chryses, 22 years, A. M. 3269

The 13th of the Theban Egyptian kings reigned Ranosis, which is Archiciator, 13 years, A. M. 3291.

The 14th of the Theban Egyptian

εβασιλευσεν Βιιρις ετη ι΄ του
δε κοσμου ην ετος ,γτδ΄.

Θηβαιων βασιλεων ιε΄ εβα-
σιλευσεν Σαωφι, Κομαστης,
κατα δε ενιους Χοηματιστης
ετη κθ΄. τουδε κοσμου ην ετος
,γτιδ΄

Θηβαιων ις΄. εβασιλευσεν
Σενσαωφις β΄. ετη ,ζ΄ του δε
κοσμου ην ετος ,γτμγ΄

Θηβαιων εβασιλευσεν Μοσ-
χερις Ἡλιοδοτος ετη λα΄. του
δε κοσμου ην ετος ,γτο΄

Θηβαιων ιη΄ εβασιλευσεν
Μουσθις ετη λγ΄. του δε κοσμου ην ετος ,γυα΄

Θηβαιων ιθ΄. εβασιλευσεν
Παμμος Αρχονδης ετη λε΄. του
δε κοσμου ην ετος ,γυλδ΄.

Θηβαιων κ΄. εβασιλευσεν
Απαππους μεγιστος, ουτος ως
φασιν παρα ωαν μιαν εβασιλευσεν ετη ρ΄. του δε κοσμου
ην ετος ,γυξθ΄.

Θηβαιων κα΄. εβασιλευσεν
Αχεσκος Οκαρας ετος α΄. του
δε κοσμου ην ετες ,γφξθ΄.

Θηβαιων κβ΄ εβασιλευσεν
Νιτωκρις αντι του ανδρος, ὁ
εστιν Αθηνα Νικηφορος, ετη
ς΄. του δε κοσμου ην ετος ,γφο΄

Θηβαιων κγ΄ εβασιλευσεν
Μυρταιος Αμμανοδοτο, ετη κβ΄.
του δε κοσμου ην ετος ,γφπς΄

Θηβαιων κδ΄ εβασιλευσεν
Θυοσιμαρης κραταιος, ὁ εστιν

kings reigned Biyris, 10 years, A M 3304.

The 15th of the Theban kings Saophis Comastes, or, according to some, Chiematistes, reigned 29 years, and A. M. 3314.

The 16th of the Theban kings Sensaophis the second, reigned 27 years, A. M 3343.

The 17th of the Theban kings, Moscheris Heliodotus, reigned 31 years, A. M 3370.

The 18th of the Theban kings, Musthis, reigned 33 years, A. M 3401.

The 19th of the Theban kings, Pammus Archondes, reigned 35 years, A. M. 3434

The 20th of the Theban kings, Apaphus Maximus, is said to have reigned 100 years with the exception of one hour, A. M. 3469

The 21st of the Theban kings, Achescus Oearas, reigned one year, A. M. 3569.

The 22nd of the Theban sovereigns was Nitocris, instead of her husband, she is Athena Nicephorus, and reigned 6 years, A. M. 3570.

The 23rd of the Theban kings, Myrtæus Ammonodotus, reigned 22 years, A. M. 3576.

The 24th of the Theban kings, Thyosimares the robust, who is called

ἥλιος, ετη ιϐ΄. τευ δε κοσμου ην
ετος ,γφϞη΄.

Θηϐαιων κε΄. εϐασιλευσεν
Θινιλλος, ὁ εστιν αυξησας το
πατριον κρατος ετη η΄. του δε
κοσμου ην ετος ,γχι΄.

Θηϐαιων κς΄. εϐασιλευσεν
Σεμφρουκρατης, ὁ εστιν Ἡρα-
/λης Ἁρποκρατης ετη ιη΄. του
δε /οσμου ετος ,γχιη΄.

Θηϐαιων κζ΄ εϐασιλευσεν
Χουθηρ Ταυρος τιραννος ετη ζ΄.
του δε κοσμου ,γχλς΄.

Θηϐαιων λη΄. εϐασιλευσεν
Μευρης Φιλοσκορος ετη ιϐ΄. του
δε ιοσμου ,γχμγ΄

Θηϐαιων ιθ΄. εϐασιλευσεν
Χομαεφθα ιοσμος Φιλεφαισ-
τος ετη ια΄ του δε κοσμου
,γχνε΄

Θηϐαιων λ΄. εϐασιλευσεν
Αγκουνιος Οχυτιραννος ετη ξ΄.
του δε νοσμου ,γχξς΄.

Θηϐαιων λα΄. εϐασιλευσεν
Πεντεαθυρις ετη μϐ΄. του δε
κοσμου ,γψκς΄.

Θηϐαιων λϐ΄. εϐασιλευσεν
Σταμενεμης ϐ΄. ετη κγ΄. του δε
κοσμου ,γψξη΄.

Θηϐαιων λγ΄. εϐασιλευσεν
Σιστοσιχερμης Ἡρακλεος κρατος ετη νε΄. του δε νοσμου,
,γψϞα΄.

Θηϐαιων λδ΄. εϐασιλευσεν
Μαρις ετη μγ΄. του δε κοσμου
,γωμς΄.

the sun, reigned 12 years, and A M
3598.

The 25th of the Theban kings,
Thinillus, which is the augmenter of
country's strength, reigned 8 years,
A. M. 3610.

The 26th of the Theban kings,
Semphrucrates, who is Hercules Har-
pocrates, reigned 18 years, A. M.
3618.

The 27th of the Theban kings,
Chuther Taurus the tyrant, 7 years,
A. M. 3636.

The 28th of the Theban kings,
Meures Philoscorus, reigned 12 years,
A. M. 3643.

The 29th of the Theban kings,
Chomaephtha Cosmus Phlephæstus,
reigned 11 years, A. M. 3655

The 30th of the Theban kings,
Ancunius Ochytyiannus, reigned ·60
years, A. M. 3666

The 31st of the Theban kings,
Penteathyris, reigned 42 years, A M.
3726.

The 32nd of the Theban kings,
Stamenemes the second, reigned 23
years, A M. 3768.

The 33rd of the Theban kings,
Sistosichermes, the strength of Hercules, reigned 55 years, A M 3791.

The 34th of the Theban kings,
Maris, reigned 43 years, A. M 3846.

Θηβαιων λε΄. εβασιλευσεν Σιφωας, ὁ και Ἑρμης υἱος Ἡφαιστου, ετη ε΄. του δε κοσμου, ͵γωπθ΄.

Θηβαιων λϛ΄. εβασιλευσεν . . . . . ετη ιδ΄. του δε κοσμου ͵γωϟδ΄.

Θηβαιων λζ΄. εβασιλευσεν Φρουρων, ητοι Νειλος, ετη ε΄. του δε κοσμου ͵γϠη΄.

Θηβαιων λη΄. εβασιλεισεν Αμουθανταιος ετη ξγ΄. του δε κοσμου ͵γϠιγ΄.

The 35th of the Theban kings, Siphoas, which is Hermes the son of Hephœstus, reigned 5 years, A. M. 3889.

The 36th of the Theban kings, ... reigned 14 years, A. M. 3894.

The 37th of the Theban kings, Phruron, which is Nilus, reigned 5 years, A. M. 3908.

The 38th of the Theban kings, Amuthantæus, reigned 63 years, A.M. 3913.—*Syncel. Chron.* 91. 96. 101. 104. 109. 123. 147.

THE FRAGMENTS

OF

THE TYRIAN ANNALS:

FROM

DIUS AND MENANDER

THE TYRIAN ANNALS:

FROM DIUS

OF HIRAM

ΑΒΙΒΑΛΟΥ τελευτησαντος, ὁ υἱος αυτον Εἱρωμος εβασιλευσεν· οὑτος τα προς ανατολας μερη της πολεως προσεχωσεν. και μειζον το αστυ πεποιη·εν, και του Ολυμπ.ου Διος το ἱερον ·αθ᾽ ἑαυτο ον εν ·ησῳ·, χωσας τον μεταξυ τοπον, σ·νηψε τη πολει, και χρυσοις αναθη·ασ·ν ε· οσμησεν αναβας δε εις τον Λιβανον ὑλοτομησε προς την των ναων κατασ·ευη·. τον δε τυραννουντα Ἱεροσολυμων Σολομωνα πεμψα. (φασι) προς τον Εἱραμον αινιγματα, και παρ᾽ αυτου λαβειν αξιουν τον δε μη δυνηθεντα δια·ρι·αι, τω λυσαντι χρη·ατα αποτινειν. ὁμωλογησ·ντα δε τον Εἱρωμον, ·αι μη δ·νηθεντα λισ·ι τα αινιγματα, πολλα ·ων χρημ·ατ··

Upon the death of Abibalus his son Hiromus succeeded to the kingdom. He raised the eastern parts of the city, and enlarged it, and joined to it the temple of Jupiter Olympius, which stood before upon an island, by filling up the intermediate space· and he adorned that temple with donations of gold· and he went up into Libanus to cut timber for the construction of the temples. And it is said that Solomon, king of Jerusalem, sent enigmas to Hiromus, and desired others in return, with a proposal that whichsoever of the two was unable to solve them, should forfeit money to the other. Hiromus agreed to the proposal, but was unable to solve the enigmas, and paid a large sum as a forfeit. And it is said that one Abdemonus, a Tyrian, solved the enigmas, and proposed others

εις το επιζημιον αναλωσαι.
ειτα δε Αβδημονον τινα Τυριον
ανδρα τα προτεθεντα λισαι
και αυτον αλλα προλαβειν α
μη λυσαντα τον Σολομωνα,
πολλα τῳ Εἰρωμω προσατοτι-
σαι χρηματα.

which Solomon was not able to un-
riddle, for which he repaid the fine
to Hiromus —*Joseph. contr. App*
lib. I c 17 —*Syncel. Chron* 182

THE TYRIAN ANNALS:

FROM MENANDER

OF HIRAM

ΓΕΛΕΥΤΗΣΑΝΤΟΣ δε Αβι-
βαλου, διεδεξατο την βασιλειαν ὁ ὑιος αυτου Εἱρωμος,
ς βιωσας ετη πεντηκοντα
ρια εβασιλευσεν ετη τρια-
οντα τεσσαρα. οὑτος εχωσε
ον Ευρυχωρον, τον τε χρυ-
ουν ϟιονα εν τοις του Διος
ενεθηκεν ετι τε ὑλην ξυλων
επελθων εκοψεν, απο του λεγο-
ϟενου, ορους Λιβανου, κεδρινα
ϟλα εις τας των ἱερων στεγας.
αθελων τε τα αρχαια ἱερα,
αινους ναους ῳκοδομησε, το
ε του Ἡρακλεους, και της
Ἀσταρτης τεμενος ανιερευσεν,
αι το μεν του Ἡρακλεους
πρωτον εποιησατο εν τῳ Περ-
τιῳ μηνι, ειτα το της Ασταρ-
ης, ὁποτε Τιτιοις επεστρα-
ευσεν, μη αποδιδουσι τους
ϟορους οὑς ϟαι ὑποταξας

AFTER the death of Abibalus, Hiromus his son succeeded him in his kingdom, and reigned thirty-four years, having lived fifty-three. He laid out that part of the city which is called Eurychoron : and consecrated the golden column which is in the temple of Jupiter. And he went up into the forest on the mountain called Libanus, to fell cedars for the roofs of the temples . and having demolished the ancient temples, he rebuilt them, and consecrated the fanes of Hercules and Astarte. he constructed that of Hercules first, in the month Peritius; then that of Astarte, when' he had overcome the Tityans who had refused to pay their tribute · and when he had reduced them he returned. In his time was a certain young man named Abdemonus, who used to solve the problems which were propounded

ἑαυτῷ π.λιν ανεστρεψεν. επι
τουτου δε τις ην Αβδημονος
παις νεωτερος, ὁς ενικα τα
προβληματα, ἀ επετασσε Σο-
λομων ὁ Ἱεροσολυμω. βασιλευς.

to him by Solomon king of Jerusalem
—*Joseph. contr App.* lib I c 18 —
Joseph. Antiq Jud lib. VIII c 5

OF THE SUCCESSORS OF HIRAM

Τελ ευτησαντος Εἱρωμου
διεδεξατο την βασιλειαν Βα-
λεαζαρος ὁ υἱος, ὁς, βιωσας
ετη τεσσαρανοντα τρια, εβασιλευσεν ετη ἑπτα. μετα τουτον Αβδαστρατος ὁ αυτου υἱος,
βιωσας ετη εινοσι εννεα, εβασιλευσεν ετη εννεα. τουτον οἱ
της τροφου αυτου υἱοι τεσσα-
ρες επιβουλευσαντες απωλεσαν,
ὡν ὁ πρεσβυτερος εβασιλευσεν
ετη δεκαδυο μεθ᾽ οὑς Ασταρ-
τος ὁ Δελαιασταρτου, ὁς, βιωσας ετη πεντηνοντα τεσσαρα,
εβασιλευσεν ετη δωδεκα. μετα
τουτον ὁ αδελφος αυτου Ασερυ·
μος, βιωσας ετη τεσσαρα και
πεντηνοντα, εβασιλευσεν ετη
εννεα οὑτος απωλετο ὑπο του
ἀδελφου Φελητος, ὁς λαβων
την βασιλειαν ηρξε μηνας
οκτω, βιωσας ετη πεντηκοντα
τουτον ανειλεν Ειθωβαλος ὁ τη,
Ασταρτης ἱερευς, ὁς, βασιλευσας ετη τριαχοντα δυο, εβια-
σεν ετη ἑξηκοντα οκτω. τουτον
διεδεξατο Βαδεζωρος υἱος, ὁς,

Upon the death of Hiromus, Balea-
zarus his son succeeded to the kingdom, he lived forty-three years, and
reigned seven · after him Abdastratus
his son reigned nine years, having
lived twenty-nine against him the
four sons of his nurse conspired, and
slew him of these the eldest reigned
twelve years · after them Astartus,
the son of Delœastartus, reigned twelve
years, having lived fifty-four · after
him his brother Aserumus reigned
nine years, having lived fifty-four .
he was slain by his brother Pheles,
who governed the kingdom eight
months, having lived fifty years . he
was slain by a priest of Astarte, Ithobalus, who reigned thirty-two years,
having lived sixty-eight · and he was
succeeded by Badezorus his son, who
reigned six years, having lived forty-
five . his successor was Matgenus his
son, who reigned nine years, having
lived thirty-two: and he was succeeded
by Phygmalion who reigned forty-seven
years, having lived fifty-six : in the
seventh year of his reign his sister

βιωσας ετη τεσσαρακοντα
πεντε, εβασιλευσεν ετη ἑξ.
τουτου διαδοχος γεγονε Ματ-
γηνος ὁ υἱος, ὁς, βιωσας ετη
τριακοντα δυο, εβασιλευσεν
ετη εννεα. τουτου διαδοχος
γεγονε Φιγμαλιων, βιωσας δ᾽
ετη πεντηκοντα ἑξ, εβασιλευσεν ετη τεσσαρακοντα ἑπτα.
εν δε τῳ επ᾽ αυτου ἑβδομῳ ετει ἡ
αδελφη αυτου φυγουσα, εν τῃ
Λιβυη πολιν ᾠκοδομησε Καρ-
χηδονα

fled from him, and founded the city of Carthage in Libya — *Joseph. contr App* lib. I c. 18.

OF THE INVASION OF SALMANASAR

Και Ελουλαιος ονομα εβασιλεισεν ετη τριακοντα ἑξ. οὑτος,
αποσταντων Κ᾽ιτταιων, ανα-
πλευσας, προσηγαγετο αυτοις
παλιν επι τουτοις πεμψας
(Σαλμανασαρ) ὁ των Ασσυ-
ριων βασιλευς, επηλθε Φοινικην
πολεμων ἁπασαν ὁς τις σπει-
σαμενος ειρηνην, μετα παντων
ανεχωρησεν οπισω απεστη τε
Τυριων Σιδων και Ακη και ἡ
Παλαι Τυρος, και πολλαι αλλαι
πολεις, αἱ τῳ των Ασσυριων
ἑαυτας βασιλει παρεδοσαν. διο
Τυριων ουχ ὑποταγεντων παλιν
ὁ βασιλευς επ᾽ αυτους ὑπε-
στραψε, Φοινικων συμπληρα-
σαντων αυτῳ ναυς ἑξηκοντα,
και επικωπους οκτακοσιοις αἱς
επιπλευσαντες οἱ Τυριοι ναυσι

Elulæus reigned thirty-six years: and he fitted out a fleet against the Cittæans (Chittim or Cypriots) who had revolted, and reduced them to obedience. But Salmanasar, the king of the Assyrians, sent them assistance, and overran Phœnicia · and when he had made peace with the Phœnicians he returned with all his forces And Sidon, and Ace (Acre), and Palæ-tyrus, and many other cities revolted from the Tyrians, and put themselves under the protection of the king of Assyria But as the Tyrians still refused to submit, the king made another expedition against them and the Phœnicians furnished him with sixty ships and eighty gallies · and the Tyrians attacked him with twelve ships, and dispersed the hostile fleet,

δεκαδιο, των νεων των αντι-
παλων διασπαρεισων, λαμβα-
νουσιν αιχμαλωτους ανδρας εις
πεντακοσιους επεταθη δη παντων εν Τυρῳ τιμη δια ταυτα
αναζευξας δ' ὁ των Ασσυριων
βασιλευς καταστησε φυλακας
επι του ποταμου και των ὑδρα-
γωγιων, οἱ διακαλυσουσι Τυριους
αρυσασθαι. και τουτο ετεσι
πεντε γενομενον, εκαρτερησαν
πινοντες εκ φρεατων ορυκτων.

and took prisoners to the amount
of five hundred men   upon which
account   the Tyrians were held in
great respect   But the king of Assyria stationed guards upon the river,
and aqueducts, to prevent the Tyrians
from drawing water : and this continued five years, during all which time
they were obliged to drink from wells
which they dug.—*Joseph Antiq. Jud.*
lib. IX. c. 14.

THE TYRIAN ANNALS.

OF THE KINGS AND JUDGES FROM NEBUCHADNEZZAR TO CYRUS

ΕΠΙ Ειθωβαλου του βασιλεως επολιορνησε Ναβουχοδονοσορος την Τιρον επ' ετη δεκατρια μετα τουτον εβασιλευσε Βααλ ετη δεκα. μετα τουτον δικασται κατεσταθησαν και εδικασαν· Εκνιβαλος Βασλαχου μηνας δυο, Χελβης Αβδαιου μηνας δεκα, Αββαρος αρχιερευς μηνας τρεις, Μυτγονος και Γεραστρατος του Αβδηλεμου δικασται ετη εξ, ων μεταξυ εβασιλευσε Βαλατορος ενιαυτον ενα· τουτου τελευτησαντος, αποστειλαντες μετεπεμψαντο Μερβαλον εν της Βαβυλωνος, και εβασιλευσεν ετη τεσσαρα τουτου τελευτησαντος, μετεπεμψαντο τον αδελφον αυτου Ειρωμον, ος εβασιλευσεν ετη εικοσιν. επι τουτου Κυρος Περσαν εδυναστευσεν.

In the reign of Ithobalus, Nabuchodonosorus besieged Tyre for thirteen years. After him reigned Baal ten years. After him Judges were appointed who judged the people. Ecnibalus, the son of Baslachus, two months; Chelbes, the son of Abdæus, ten months. Abbarus, the high-priest, three months: Mytgonus and Gerastratus the son of Abdelemus, six years. after them Balatorus reigned one year. After his death they sent to fetch Merbalus from Babylon; and he reigned four years. and when he died they sent for Hiromus, his brother, who reigned 20 years. In his time Cyrus was king of Persia.—*Joseph contr App* lib I c. 21

THE ORACLES

OF

ZOROASTER.

THE ORACLES

OF

ZOROASTER.

ΤΑ ΤΟΥ ΖΩΡΟΑΣΤΡΟΥ ΛΟΓΙΑ.

ΜΟΝΑΣ ΔΥΑΣ ΚΑΙ ΤΡΙΑΣ

. . . . . Ὅπου πατρικη μονας εστι.

Ταναη εστι μονας . . . . ἡ δυο γεννᾳ

Δυας γαρ παρα τῳ δε καθηται, και νοεραις αςραπ7ει τομαις

Και το ʌυβερνᾳν τα παντα, και ταττειν ἑʌαστον ου ταχθεν

Παντι γαρ εν κοσμῳ λαμπει τριας, ἡς μονας

   αρχει.

Αρχη πασης τμησεως ἡ δε ἡ ταξις.

Εις τρια γαρ νους ειπε πατρος τεμνεσθαι ἁπαντα,

Οὑ το θελειν κατενευσε, και ἡδη παντα ετετμητο

Εις τρια γαρ ειπε ʌους πατρος αιδιου,

Νῳ παντα κυβερνων.

Και εφανησαν εν αυτη ἡ τ᾽ αρετη, και ἡ σοφια.

Και ἡ πολυφρων ατρεκεια.

Τη τωνδε ῥεει τριαδος δεμας προ της ουσης,

Ου πρωτης, αλʌ᾽ οὑ τα μετρειται.

Αρχαις γαρ τρισι ταις δε λαβοις δουλευειν ἁπαντα

. . . . Ἱερʌς πρωτος δρομος, εν δ᾽ αρα μεσσῳ.

Ηεριος, τριτος αλʌος, ὁς εν πυρι την χθοʌα θαλπει.

Και πηγη πηγωʌ, και πηγωʌ . . απασων.

Μητρα συνεχουσα τα παντα

Ἐνθεν αρδην θρωσκει γενεσις πολυποικιλου ὑλης.

THE ORACLES OF ZOROASTER.

MONAD, DUAD, AND TRIAD

. . Where the paternal Monad is
The Monad is enlarged, and generates two,
For the Duad sits by him, and glitters with intellectual Sections
Both to govern all things, and to order every thing not ordered
For in the whole world shineth the Triad, over which the Monad
    rules.
This order is the beginning of all section
For the mind of the Father said, that all things be cut into three:
Whose will assented, and then all things were divided.
For the mind of the Eternal Father said all things into three,
Governing all things by the mind.
And there appeared in it (the Triad) virtue, and wisdom,
And multiscient verity
This way floweth the shape of the Triad, being pre-existent.
Not the first (Essence) but where they are measured.
For thou must conceive that all things serve these three principles
The first is the sacred course . . . but in the middle
An, the third the other which cherisheth the earth in fire
The fountain of fountains and . . . of all fountains
The matrix containing all things
Thence abundantly springs forth the generation of multifarious
    matter

Ενθεν συρομενος πρηστηρ αμυδροιο πυρος ανθος,
Κοσμων ενθρωσκων κοιλωμασι. Παντα γαρ ενθεν
Αρχεται εις το κατω τεινειν ακτινας αγητας.

ΠΑΤΗΡ ΚΑΙ ΝΟΥΣ.

Έαυτον δ πατηρ ήρπασεν ουδ' εν έη
Δυναμει νοερα κλεισας ιδιον πυρ.
Ου γαρ απο πατρικης αρχης ατελες τι τροχαζει.
Παντα γαρ εξετελεσε πατηρ,
Και νῳ παρεδωκε ευτερῳ,
Ὁν πρωτον κληιζεται παν γενος ανδρων.
Πατρογενες φαος, πολυ γαρ μοιος
Εκ πατρος αλκης δρεψαμενος νοου ανθος
Εργα νοησας, γαρ πατρικος νοος αυτογενεθλος,
Πασιν ενεσπειρε δεσμον πυριβριθη ερωτος
Οφρα τα παντα μενη, χρονον εις απεραντον ερωντα
Μητε πασι τα πατρος νοερας ὑφασμενα
              φεγγει
Ὡς εν ερωτι μενη κοσμου στοιχεια μενοντα.
Εχει τῳ νοειν πατρικον νουν ενδιδοναι
Πασαις πηγαις τε και αρχαις
Εστι γαρ περας του πατρικου βαθου, και πηγη των
              νοερων
Μη δε προηλθεν, αλλ' εμενεν εν τῳ πατρικῳ βαθῳ,
Και εν τῳ αδυτῳ, κατα την θεοθρεμμονα σιγην
Ου γαρ εις ὑλην, πυρ επεκεινα το πρωτον
Εην δυναμιν κατανλειει εργοις, αλλα νοῳ
Συμβολα γαρ πατρινος νοος εσπειρε κατα κοσμον
Ὁς τα νοητα νοει και αφραστα καλληιται.
Ὁλοφυης μερισμος, και αμεριστος
Νῳ μεν κατεχει τα νοητα, αισθησιν δ' επαγει
              κοσμοις
Νῳ μεν κατεχει τα νοητα, ψυχην δ' επαγει κοσμοις

Thence extracted a Prester the flower of glowing fire,
Flashing into the cavities of the World: For all things from thence
Begin to extend downward their admirable beams

THE FATHER AND MIND

The Father hath snatched away himself, neither
Hath he shut up his own fire in his intellectual power.
For nothing unfinished proceedeth from the Father's rule.
For the Father perfected all things,
And delivered them over to the second mind,
Which the whole race of men call the first
Light begotten of the Father, for he alone
Having cropt the flower of the Mind from the Father's vigor
For the paternal self-begotten Mind understanding (his) work,
Sowed in all the fiery bond of Love,
That all things might continue loving for ever.
Neither those things which are intellectually context in the Light
    of the Father in all things
That being the Elements of the World they might persist in Love
For by understanding he hath the power to instil the paternal mind
Into all fountains and beginnings
For it is the bound of the Paternal depth and the fountain of
    the Intellectuals
Neither went he forth, but abode in the Paternal depth,
And in the Adytum according to divinely-nourished Silence.
For the fire once above, shutteth not his power
Into matter by Actions, but by the Mind.
For the Paternal Mind hath sowed symbols through the world.
Which understandeth intelligibles and beautifieth ineffables.
Wholly division and indivisible
By mind he contains the Intelligibles, but introduceth sense into
    the Worlds.
By mind he contains the Intelligibles, but introduceth Soul into
    the Worlds.

ΝΟΥΣ, ΝΟΗΤΑ, ΚΑΙ ΝΟΕΡΑ.

Και του ένος γου του νοητου.

Ου γαρ ανευ νοος εστι νοητου· οι χωρις ὑπαρχει.

Τα μεν εστι νοερα και νοητα, όσα νοουντα
      νοειται.

Τροφη δε τω νοωιτι το ,οητον.

Μανθανε το νοητον, επει νοου εξω ὑπαρχει

Και του νου, ὁς τον εμπυριον κοσμον αγει

Νου γαρ νους εστιν ὁ κοσμου τεχνιτης πυριοι.

Οἱ τον ἱπερκοσμον πατρινοι βυθον ιστε νοοιντες

Ἡ νοητη πασης τμησεως αγει.

Εστι γαρ τι νοητον, ὁ χρη σε νοειν νοου
      ανθει

Ἡ γαρ επεγνλινη, ὡς αν νοιν, κακεινο νοησῃ,

Ὡς τι νοων, ου λεινον
      νοησεις

Εστ. γαρ αλνης αμριφαους δυναμις,

Νοεραις στραπτοισα τομαισι, ου δη χρη

Σφοδροτητι νοειν το νοητον εκεινο.

Αλλα νοου ταναου ταναη φλογι

Παντα μετροισῃ, πλην το νοητον εκεινο

Χρεω δη τουτο νοησαι· η γαρ επεγκλινης

Σον νουν, νακεινο νησεις ουκ ακτενως

Αλλ' ἁγνον επιστροφον ομμα,

Φεροντα σης ψυχης τειναι κενεον νοον

Εις το νοητον, οφρα μαθῃς το νοητον·

Επει εξω νοου ὑπαρχει.

Τον δε νυει πας νους Θεον, ου γαρ
      ανει

Νοος εστι νοητοι, και το νοητον οι νου χωρις ὑπαρχει.

Τοις δε πυρος νοερου νοεροις πρηστησιν ἁπαντα

Ειναθε δουλευοντα, πατρος πειθηνιδι βουλῃ

MIND, INTELLIGIBLES, AND INTELLECTUALS.

And of the one Mind, the Intelligible (Mind)

For the Mind is not without the Intelligible; it exists not without it.

These are Intellectuals and Intelligibles which being understood
    understand.

For the Intelligible is the aliment of the Intelligent.

Learn the Intelligible, since it exists beyond the Mind

And of the Mind which moves the empyreal heaven

For the Framer of the fiery world is the Mind of the Mind.

You who know certainly the supermundane paternal depth.

The Intelligible is predominant over all section.

There is something Intelligible which it behoves thee to under-
    stand with the flower of the Mind.

For if thou inclinest thy mind, thou shalt understand this also

Yet understanding something (of it) thou shalt not understand
    this wholly,

For it is a power of circumlucid strength,

Glittering with intellectual sections (rays) : but it behoves not

To consider this Intelligible with vehemence of Intellection,

But with the ample flame of the ample Mind

Which measureth all things, except this Intelligible :

But it behoves to understand this, for if thou inclinest

Thy mind thou shalt understand this also, not fixedly

But having a pure turning eye (thou must)

Extend the empty mind of thy soul

Towards the Intelligible; that thou mayest learn the Intelligible;

For it exists beyond the mind

But every mind understands this God, for the Mind is not

Without the Intelligible, neither is the Intelligible without the
    Mind.

To the Intellectual Presters of the intellectual fire all things

By yielding are subservient to the persuasive counsel of the Father,

Και το νοειν, αει τε μενειν αολνω στροφαλιγγι.

Πηγας τε και αρχας, δινειν, αε. τε μενειν αολιω
         στροφαλιγγι

Αλλα δ' οιομα σεμνον ακοιμητ;'
         στροφαλιγγι

Κοσμοις ενθρωσκων, κρεπιην δια πατρος εν.πην.

'Υπο δυο νοαν ἡ ζωογονος πηγη περιεχεται
         ψυχων.

Και ὁ ποιητης, ὁς αυτουργων τεκτηνατο τον κοσμον.

'Ος εκ νοου εκθωρε πρωτος.

Εσσαμενος πιρι πυρ, συνδεσμων οφρα κερασῃ

Πηγαιους κρατηρας, ἑου πυρος ανθος επισχων.

Νοεραις αςραπτει τομαις, ερωτος δ'ενεπλησε τα
         παντα

Τα ατυπωτα τυπουσθαι

Σμηνεσσιν εοικυιαι φερονται, ῥηγνυμεναι

Κοσμου περι σωμασι

'Α νους λεγει, τῳ νοειν δη που λεγει.

'Η μεν γαρ δυναμις συν εκεινοις, ιους δ' απ' εκεινου.

ΙΥΓΓΕΣ, ΙΔΕΑΙ ΑΡΚΑΙ.

Πολλαι μεν αἱδε επεμβαινουσι φαεινοις κοσμοις.

Ενθρωσκουσαι, και εν αἱς ακροτητες εασι τρεις,

'Υποκειται αυταις αρχιος αυλων.

Αρχας, αἱ πατρος εργα νοησασαι
         νοητα

Αισθητοις εργοις, και σωμασιν αφεναλιψεν

Δια πορθμιοι ἑστωτες φαναι τῳ πατρι και τη ὑλη.

Και τα εμφανη μιμηματα των αφανων εργαζομενοι.

Και τ' αφανη εις την εμφανη κοσμοποιιαν εγγραφοντες.

Νους πατρος ερροιζησε, νοησας ακμαδι
         βουλη

Παμμορφους ιδεας. πηγης δ' απο μιας αποπτασαι

Εξεθορον. πατροθεν γαρ εην βουλη τε τελος τε

And to understand, and always to remain in a restless whirling.

Fountains and principles, to turn, and always to remain in a
restless whirling

By insinuating into Worlds the venerable name in a sleepless
whirling

By reason of the terrible menace of the Father

Under two Minds the life-generating fountain of the Souls is
contained

And the Maker who, self-operating, framed the World.

Who sprung first out of the Mind

Clothing fire with fire, binding them together to mingle

The fountainous craters, preserving the flower of his own fire

He glittereth with Intellectual sections, and filleth all things with
love

That things unfashioned may be fashioned.

Like swarms they are carried, being broken

About the bodies of the world.

What the Mind speaks, it speaks by understanding.

Power is with them—mind is from her

IYNGLS, IDEAS, AND PRINCIPLES.

These being many ascend into the lucid Worlds,

Springing into them, and in which are three tops.

Beneath them lies the chief of Immaterials

Principles, which have understood the intelligible works of the
Father,

Disclosed them in sensible works as in bodies :

Being (as it were) the ferrymen betwixt the Father and matter

And producing manifest images of unmanifest things :

And inscribing the unmanifest in the manifest frame of the World

The Mind of the Father made a jarring noise, understanding by
vigorous counsel

Omniform Ideas : and flying out of one fountain

They sprung forth . for from the Father was the counsel and end

P

Δι' ὧν συναπτεται τῳ πατρι, αλλην κατ' αλλην
Ζωην, απο μεριζομενων οχετων
Αλλ' εμερεισθησαν, νοερῳ πυρι μοιρηθεισαι
Εις αλλας νοερας· κοσμῳ γαρ αναξ
   πολυμορφῳ
Προυθηκεν νοερον τυπον αφθιτον, ου κατα κοσμον
Ιχνος επειγομενος μορφης καθ' ἁ κοσμος
   εφανθη,
Παντοιαις ιδεαις κεχαρισμενος, ὦν μια πηγη,
Εξ ἡς ῥοιξουνται μεμερισμεναι αλλαι,
Απλατοι, ῥηγνυμεναι κοσμου περι σωματι·
Αἱ περι κολπους σμερδαλεους, σμηνεσσιν εοικυιας,
Φορεονται τραπουσαι περι δ' αμφι αλλυδις αλλη.
Εννοιαι νοεραι πηγης πατρικης απο
Πολυ δραττομεναι πυρος ανθος
Ακοιμητου χρονου, ανμη αρχεγονου ιδεας
Πρωτη πατρος εβλισε τας δ' αυτοθαλης πηγη.
Νοουμεναι ιυγγες πατροθεν νοεουσι και αυται.
Βουλαις αφθεγκτοισι κινουμεναι ὡστε νοησαι

῾ΕΚΑΤΗ, ΣΥΝΟΧΕΙΣ, ΚΑΙ ΤΕΛΕΑΡΧΑΙ

Εξ αυτου γαρ παντες ενθρωσκουσι
Αμειλικτοι τε κεραυνοι, και πρηστηροδοχοι κολποι
Παμφεγγεος αλκης πατρογενους ῾Εκατης.
Και ὑπεζωκος πυρος ανθος, ἡ δε κραταιον
Πνευμα πολων, πυριων επεκεινα
Φρουρειν αυ πρηστηρσιν ἑοις ακροτητας εδωκεν
Εγκερασας αλκης ιδιον μενος εν συνοχευσιν
Ω τας εχει κοσμος νοερους ανοχηας απαμπεις
῾Οτι εργατις, ὁτι εκδοτις εστι πυρος
   ζωηφορου
῾Οτι και το ζωογονον πληροι της ῾Εκατης κολπον
Και επιρρει τοις συνοχευσιν αλκην ζηδωρον πυρα,
Μεγα δυναμενοιο

By which they are connected with the Father by alternate
Life from several vehicles.
But they were divided, being by intellectual fire distributed
Into other Intellectuals · for the king did set before the multiform
    world
An intellectual incorruptible pattern, the print of whose form
He promoted through the world, according to which things the
    world appeared
Beautified with all kinds of Ideas, of which there is one fountain;
Out of which come rushing forth others undistributed,
Being broken about the bodies of the World;
Which through the vast recesses, like swarms,
Are carried round about every way
Intellectual notions from the paternal fountain
Cropping the flower of Fire
In the point of sleepless time of this primigeneous Idea
The first self-budding fountain of the Father budded.
Intelligent Iynges do (themselves) also understand from the Father.
By unspeakable counsels being moved so as to understand.

HECATE, SYNOCHES, AND TELETARCHS.

For out of him spring all
Implacable thunders, and the prester-receiving cavities
Of the entirely-lucid strength of Father-begotten Hecate.
And he who begirds (viz.) the flower of Fire and the strong
Spirit of the poles fiery above
He gave to his presters that they should guard the tops.
Mingling the power of his own strength in the Synoches
Oh how the world hath intellectual guides inflexible!
Because she is the operatrix, because she is the dispensatrix of
    fire-giving life.
Because also it fills the life-producing bosom of Hecate,
And instils in the Synoches the enlivening strength
Of potent fire.

Αλλα και φρουρο. των εργων εισι του πατρο .
Αφομοιοι γαρ ἑαυτον, ελεινος επιγομενος
Τον τυπον περιβαλλεσθαι των ειδωλων.
Οἱ τελεταρχαι συνειληπται τοις συνοχευσι.
Τοις δε πυρος νοεσου νοεραις πρηστηρσιν
Ἀπαντα εικαθε δουλειοντα
Αλλα και ὑλαιοις ὁσα δουλευει συνοχευσι
Ἑσσαμενου παντευχον αλκην φωτος κελαδοντος.
Αλκη τριγλιχω, νοον ψυχην θ' ὁπλισαντα
Παντοιαδος συνθημα βαλλειν φρενι
Μηδ' επιφοιταν εμπυριοις σποραδην οχετοις,
Αλλα στιβαρηδον.
Οἱ δε τα ατομα, και αισθητα δημιουργουσι,
Και σωματοειδη, και κατατεταγμενα εις Ὑλην.

ΨΥΧΗ, ΦΥΣΙΣ.

Ὁτι ψυχη πυρ δυναμει πατρος ουσα φαεινον,
Αθανατος τε μενει, και ζωης δεσποτις εστι
Και ισχει κοσμου πολλα πληρωματα κολπων
Νου γαρ μιμημα πελει, το δε τεχθεν εχει τι
          σωματος
Μιγνυμενων δ' οχετων, πυρος αφθιτου εργα
          τελουσα
Μετα δε πατρικας διανοιας ψυχη, εγω, ναιω
Θερμη, ψυχουσα τα παντα, κατεθετο γαρ
Νουν μεν ενι ψυχη, ψυχην δ' ενι σωματι αργω
Ἡμεων εγκατεθηκε πατηρ ανδρων τε Θεων τε.
Αρδην εμψυχοισα φαος, πυρ, αιθερα, κοσμους
Συνυφισταται γαρ τα φυσικα εργα τω νοερω φεγγει
Του πατρος· Ψυχη γαρ κοσμησασα τον μεγαν
Ουρανον, και κοσμουσα μετα του πατρος
Κερατα δε και αυτης εστηρικται ανω.
Νωτοις δ' αμφι θεας φυσις απλετος
          ηωρηται

But they are guardians of the works of the Father
For he assimilates himself, professing
To be clothed with the print of the images
The Teletarchs are comprehended with the Synoches.
To those intellectual presters of intellectual fire
All things are subservient.
But as many as serve the material Synoches
Having put on the completely-armed vigour of resounding light
With triple strength fortifying the soul and the mind
To put into the mind the symbol of variety.
And not to walk dispersedly on the empyreal channels
But firmly.
These frame indivisibles and sensibles,
And corporiforms and things destined to matter

SOUL, NATURE

The Soul being a bright fire, by the power of the Father,
Remains immortal and is mistress of life,
And possesseth many complexions of the cavities of the world :
For it is an imitation of the Mind ; but that which is born hath
    something of the body.
The channels being intermixed she performs the part of incor-
    ruptible fire.
Next the paternal conception, I, the soul dwell,
Warmth heating all things, for he did put
The mind in the soul, the soul in the dull body
Of us the father of gods and men interposed.
Abundantly animating light, fire, ether, worlds
For natural works co-exist with the intellectual light
Of the Father   For the soul which adorned the great
Heaven, and adorning with the Father,
But her horns are fixed above
But about the shoulders of the Goddess immense Nature is
    exalted.

Αρχει δ' αυ φυσις ακαματη κοσμων τε και εργων·
Ουρανος οφρα θεει δρομον αιδιον κατασυρων·
Και ταχυς ἡελιος περι κεντρον, ὁπας εθας ελθη.
Μη φυσεας εμβλεψεις εἱμαρμενον οινομα τησδε.

ΚΟΣΜΟΣ.

Ὁ ποιητης ὁς αυτουργων τεκτηνατο τον κοσμον.
Και τις πυρος ογκος εην ἑτερος· τα δε παντα
Αυτουργαν, ἱνα σωμα το κοσμικον εκτοτυπειθη
Κοσμος ἰν' εκδηλος, και μη φαινηται ὑμελωδης
Τον ὁλον κοσμον εκ πυρος, και ἑδατος, και γης,
Και παντοτροφον αιθρης
Τ'αρβητα, και τα ρητα συνθηματα του κοσμου.
Αλλην κατ' αλλην ζωην, απο μεριζαμενων οχετων
Αλαθεν διηκοντος επι το κατ' αντικρι
Δια του κεντρου της γης, και πεμπτον μεσον, αλλον
Πυριοχον, ευθα κατεισι μεχρι ὑλαιων οχετων
Ζωηφορον πυρ
Κεντρω επισπερχων ἑαυτον φωτος κελαδοντος
Πηγαιον αλλον, ὁς τον εμπιριον νοσμον αγει
Κεντρον αφ' οὑ πασαι μεχρις αν τυχον ισαι εασι.
Συμβολα γαρ πατρικος νοος εσπειρε κατα κοσμον.
Μεσον των πατεραν ἑκαστης κεντρον φορειται
Νου γαρ μιμημα πελει το δε τεχθεν εχει τι
   σωματος

ΟΥΡΑΝΟΣ.

Ἑπτα γαρ εξωγκασε πατηρ στερεωματα κοσμων
Τον ουρανον κυρτω σχηματι περικλεισας·
Πηξε δε πολυν ὁμιλον αστερων απλανων
Ζαων και πλανωμενον ὑρεστηκεν ἑπταδα
Γην δ' εν μεσω τιθεις, ὑδωρ δ' εν γαιας κολποις,

Again indefatigable Nature commands the worlds and works;
That Heaven drawing an eternal course might run,
And the swift sun might come about the centre as he useth
Look not into the fatal name of this Nature

THE WORLD

The Maker who operating by himself framed the World.
And there was another bulk of fire, self-operating
All things, that the body of the World might be perfected.
That the World might be manifest, and not seem membranous.
The whole World of fire, and water, and earth,
And all-nourishing ether
The inexpressible and expressible watchwords of the World
One life with another, from the distributed channels
Passing from above through the opposite part
Through the centre of the Earth, and another fifth the middle,
Another fiery channel, where it descends to the material channels
Life-bringing fire
Stirring himself up with the goad of resounding light
Another fountainous, which guides the empyreal World.
The centre from which all (lines) which way soever are equal
For the paternal Mind sowed symbols through the World
For the centre of every one is carried betwixt the Fathers
For it is an imitation of the Mind, but that which is born hath
    something of the Body.

HEAVEN

For the Father congregated seven firmaments of the World,
Circumscribing Heaven in a round figure
And fixed a great company of inerratic stars
And he constituted a septenary of erratic animals
Placing earth in the middle, and water in the middle of the earth,

Ηερα δ' αιωθεν τουτων

Πηξε δε και πολυν ὁμιλον αστερων απλανων.

Μη τασει επιτονῳ πονηρᾳ

Πηξη δε πλανην οιν εχουση φερεσθαι

Επηξε δε και πολυν ὁμιλον αστερων απλανων

Το πυρ προς το πυρ αναγκασας

Πηξη πλανην ουκ εχουση φερεσθαι

Ἐξ αυτοις ὑ—εστησεν, ἑβδομον ἡελιοι,

Μετεμβολησας πιρ

Το αταχ—ον αιτων ευταντοις ανακρεμασας ζωναις.

Τικτει γαρ ἡ θεα, ἡελιον τε μεγαν κα. λαμπραν σεληνην.

Αιθηρ, ἡλιε, πνευμα σεληνης, αερος αγοι.

Ἡλιαιαν τε κινλιν, και μηναιων ναλαχισμων

Κολπαν τε ηεριαν

Αιθρης μελος, ἡελιου τε, και μηνης οχεταν. ἡ τε
         ηερος

Και πλατις αηρ, μηναιος τε δρομος, και πολος ἡελιοιο.

Συλλεγει αυτο, λαμβανουσα αιθρης μελος,

Ἡελιου τε, σεληνης τε, και ὁσα ηερι
         σινεχονται

Πυρ πυρος εξοχετευμα, και πυρος ταμιας

Χαιται γαρ ες οξυ πεφυκοτι φωτι βλετονται,

Ενθα Κροονς.

Ἡελιος παρεδρος επισκοπεων πολον αγνον

Αιθεριος τε δρομος και μηνης απλετος ὁρμη,

Ηεριοι τε ῥοαι

Ἡελιον τε μεγαν, και λαμπραν σεληνην

ΧΡΟΝΟΣ.

Θεον εγκοσμιον, αιανιον, απεραντον.

Νεον και πρεσβυτην, ἑλικοειδη

Και πηγαιον αλιον, ὁς τον εμπιριον κοσμον αγει.

The air above these.

He fixed a great company of inerratic stars,
To be carried not by laborious and troublesome tension,
But by a settlement which hath no error
He fixed a great company of inerratic stars,
Forcing fire to fire.
To be carried by a settlement which hath no error.
He constituted them six, casting into the midst
The seventh fire of the sun.
Suspending their disorder in well-ordered zones.
For the goddess brings forth the great sun and the bright moon
Oh ether, sun, spirit of the moon, guides of the air,
And of the solar circles, and of the lunar clashings
And of the aerial recesses!
The melody of the ether, and of the passages of the sun and
  moon, and of the air.
And the wide air, and the lunar course, and the pole of the sun,
It collects it, receiving the melody of the ether,
And of the sun, and of the moon, and of all things that are
  contained in the air
Fire the derivation of fire, and the dispenser of fire.
His hair pointed is seen by his native light,
Hence Cronus.
The sun assessor beholding the pure pole
And the ethereal course and the vast motion of the moon,
And the aerial fluxions.
And the great sun, and the bright moon.

TIME

The mundane god eternal, infinite.
Young and old, and of a spiral form,
And another fountainous who guides the empyreal heaven.

ΨΥΧΗ, ΣΩΜΑ, ΑΝΘΡΩΠΟΣ.

Χρη σε σπευδειν προς το φαος και πατρος αυγας,
Ενθεν επεμφθη σοι ψυχη, πολυν εσσαμενη νουν
Ταυτα πατηρ εννοησε, βροτος δ' οι εψυχωτο.
Συμβολα γαρ πατρικος νοος εσπειρε ταις ψυχαις,
Ερωτι βαθει αναπλησας την ψυχην.
Κατεθετο γαρ νουν εν ψυχη, εν σωματι δε
Ὑμεας εγκατεθηκε πατηρ ανδρων τε θεων τε.
Ασωματα μεν εστι τα θεια παντα
Σωματα δ' εν αυτοις ὑμων ἑνεκεν ενδεδεται.
Μη δυναμενους κατασχειν ασωματος των σωματων,
Δια την σωματικην, εις ἡν ενεκεντρισθητε, φυσιν
Εν δε θεω κεινται πυρσους ἑλκουσαι ακμαιους
Εκ πατροθεν κατιοντες, αφ' ὡν ψυχη κατιοντων
Εμπυριων δρεπεται καρπων, ψυχοτροφον ανθος.
Διο και νοησασαι τα εργα του πατρος
Μοιρης ειμαρμενης το πτερον φευγουσιν αναιδες
Καν γαρ τηνδε ψυχην ιδης αποκαταστασαν,
Αλλ' αλλην ενιησι πατηρ, εναριθμιον ειναι
Ἡ μαλα δε κειναι γε μακαρταται εξοχα πασεων
Ψυχαων, ποτι γαιαν απ' ουρανοθεν προχεονται.
Κειναι ολβιαι τε, και ου φατα νειματα εχουσαι
Ὁσσαι απ' αιγληεντος, αναξ, σεθεν, η δε και αυτου
Εκ Διος εξεγενοντο, μιτου κρατερης ὑπ' αναγκης,
Ἡγεισθα ψυχης βαθος αμβροτον, ομματα δ'
            αρδην
Παντα εκπετασον ανω
Μητε κατω νευσεις εις τον μελαναυγεα κοσμον.
Ὡ βαθος αιεν απιστος ὑπεστρωται τε, και Ἁδης
Αμφικνεφης, ῥιπων, ειδωλοχαρης, ανοητος,
Κρημνωδης, σκολιος, πωρον βαθος αιεν ἑλισσων,
Λει νυμφευων αφανες δεμας, αργον, απνευμον.

SOUL, BODY, MAN.

It behoves thee to hasten to the light, and the beams of the Father,
From whence was sent to thee a Soul clothed with much Mind.
These things the Father conceived, and so the mortal was animated
For the paternal Mind sowed symbols in Souls,
Replenishing the Soul with profound love.
For the Father of Gods and Men placed the Mind in the Soul,
And in the Body he established you
For all divine things are incorporeal.
But bodies are bound in them for your sakes
Incorporeals not being able to contain the bodies
By reason of the corporeal nature in which you are concentrated.
And they are in God, attracting strong flames.
Descending from the Father, from which descending the Soul
Crops of empyreal fruits the soul-nourishing flower.
And therefore conceiving the works of the Father
They avoid the audacious wing of fatal destiny
And though you see this soul manumitted,
Yet the Father sends another to make up the number.
Certainly these are superlatively blessed above all
Souls, they are sent forth from heaven to earth.
And those rich souls, which have inexpressible fates,
As many of them (O king) as proceed from shining thee,
Or from Jove himself, under the strong power of his thread,
Let the immortal depth of thy Soul be predominant; but thine
    eyes
Extend upwards
Stoop not down to the dark world.
Beneath which continually lies a faithless depth and Hades
Dark all over, squalid, delighting in images unintelligible,
Precipitous, craggy, always involving a dark abyss,
Always espousing an opacous, idle, breathless body.

Και ὁ μισοφανης κοσμος, και τα σκολια ῥειθρα
'Υφ' ὡν πολλοι κατασειρονται.
Ζητησον παραδεισον.
Διζεο συ ψυχης οχετον, ὁθεν, η τινι ταξει
Σωματι τιθυσας, επι ταξιν αφ' ἡς
    ερῥυης
Αυθις αναστησεις, ἱερῳ λογῳ εργον ἑνωσας.
Μητε κατω νευσεις, κρημνος κατα γης ὑποκειται
'Επταπορου συρων κατα βαθμιδος· ἡν
    ὑπο
Δεινης αναγκης θρονος εστι.
Μη συ αυξανε την εἱμαρμενην.
Ψυχη ἡ μεροπων θεον αγξει πως εις ἑαυτην.
Ουδεν θνητον εχουσα, ὁλη θεοθεν μεμεθευσται.
'Αρμονιαν αυχει γαρ, ἱφ' ἡ πελε σωμα βροτειον.
Εκτεινας πυρινον νουν εργον επ' ευσεβιης,
'Ρευστον και σωμα σαωσεις
Εστι και ειδωλῳ μερις εις τοπον αμφιφαοντα
Παντοθεν ατλαστῳ ψυχη πυρος ἡνια τεινον
'Η πυριθαλπης εννοια πρωτιστην εχει ταξιν.
Τῳ πυρι γαρ βροτος εμπελασας θεοθεν φαος ἑξει
Δηθυνοντι γαρ βροτῳ κρεπνοι μακαρες τελεθουσι
Αἱ ποιναι μεροπων αγκτειραι.
Και τα κακης ὑλης βλαστηματα χρηστα, και εσθλα
Ελπις τρεφετω σε πυριοχος αγγελικῳ ενι χαρῳ
Αλλ' ουκ εισδεχεται κεινης το θελειν πατριος νους,
Μεχρις αν εξελθῃ ληθης, και ῥημα λαλησῃ
Μνημην εισθεμενη πατρικου συνθηματος αγνου.
Τοις δε διδακτον φαους εδωκε γνωρισμα λαβεσθαι
Τους δε ὑπνωοντας ἑης ενεναρπισεν αλκης
Μη πνευμα μολινης μητε βαθυνῃς το επιπεδον.
Μητε το της ὑλης συβαλον κρημνῳ καταλειψεις
Μη εξαξης, ἱνα μη εξιουσα εχῃ τι.
Βιῃ ὁτι σωμα λιποντων ψυχαι καθαρωταται.
Ψυχης εξωστηρες αναπνοοι, ευλυτοι
    εισι

And the light-hating world, and the winding currents
By which many things are swallowed up.
Seek Paradise.
Seek thou the way of the Soul, whence, and by what order
Having served the body, to the same place from which thou didst
    flow,
Thou mayest rise up again, joining action to sacred speech.
Stoop not down, for a precipice lies below the Earth.
Drawing through the ladder which hath seven steps; beneath
    which
Is the throne of necessity
Enlarge not thy destiny
The Soul of men will in a manner clasp God to herself
Having nothing mortal she is wholly inebriated from God
For she boasts harmony, in which the mortal body exists
If thou extend the fiery mind to the work of piety,
Thou shalt preserve the fluxible body
There is a room for the image also in the circumlucid place.
Every way to the unfashioned soul stretch the reins of fire
The fire-glowing cogitation hath the first rank.
For the mortal approaching to the fire shall have light from God
For to the slow mortal the Gods are swift.
The furies are stranglers of men
The bourgeons even of ill matter are profitable and good.
Let fiery hope nourish thee in the angelic region,
But the paternal Mind accepts not her will,
Until she go out of oblivion and pronounce a word
Inserting the remembrance of the pure paternal symbol.
To these he gave the docile character of life to be comprehended
Those that were asleep he made fruitful by his own strength.
Defile not the spirit nor deepen a superficies
Leave not the dross of matter on a precipice.
Bring her not forth, lest going forth she have something.
The souls of those who quit the body violently are most pure
The ungirders of the soul which give her breathing are easy to be
    loosed.

Λαιησ' εν λαγοσιν Ἑκατης αρετης τελε πηγη·
Ενδον ὁλη μιμνουσα, το παρθενον ου προιεισα.
Ω τολμηροτατης φυσεως, ανθρωπε, τεχνασμα,
Μη τα τελωρια μετρα γαιης ὑπο σην φρενα βαλλου,
Ου γαρ αληθειης φυτον ενι χθονι.
Μητε μετρει μετρα ἡελιου κανονας συναθροισας,
Αιδιῳ βουλη φερεται, ουχ ἑνεκα σοιο.
Μηναιων μεν δρομημα, και αστεριον
                προπορευμα
Μηνης ῥοιζον εασον, αει τρεχει εργῳ αναγκης
Αστεριον προπορευμα, σεθεν χαριν ουκ ελοχευθη
Αιθεριος ορνιθων ταρσος πλατις ου ποτ' αληθης,
Ου θυσιαν σπλαγχναν τε τομαι ταδ' αθυρματα παντα,
Εμπορικης απατης στηριγματα φευγε συ ταυτα
Μελλων ευσεβιης ἱερον παραδεισον ανοιγειν
Ενθ' αρετη, σοφια τε, και εινομια συναγονται
Σον γαρ αγγειον θηρες χθονος οικησουσι.
Αυτους δε χθων νατωρικται ες τεκνα μεχρις.

ΔΑΙΜΟΝΕΣ, ΤΕΛΕΤΑΙ

Ἡ φυσις πειθει ειναι τοις δαιμονας αγνους.
Και τα κακης ὑλης βλαστηματα χρηστα, και εσθλα.
Αλλα ταυτα εν αβατοις σηκοις διανοιας ανελιττω
Πυρ ικελον σκιρτηδον επ' ηερος οιδμα τιταινων,
Η και πυρ ατυπωτον, ὁθεν φωνην ποθθεουσαν,
Η φως πλουσιον, αμφιγειην ῥοιζαιον, ελιχθεν·
Αλλα και ἱππον ιδειν φωτος πλεον αστραπτοντα,
Η και παιδα θεοις νωτοις εποχουμενον ἱππου,
Εμπυρον η χρυσῳ πεπυκασμενον, η παλιγυμνον,
Η και τοξευοντα, και εστωτα επι νωτοις,
Πολλακις ην λεξης μοι, αθρησης παντα
                λεοντα,
Ουτε γαρ ουρανιος κυρτος τοτε φαινεται ογκος
Αστερες ου λαμπουσι, το μηνης φας νεκαλυπται,

In the side of sinister Hecate there is a fountain of virtue,
Which remains entire within, not omitting her virginity
Oh man, the machine of boldest nature!
Subject not to thy mind the vast measures of the earth,
For the plant of truth is not upon earth.
Nor measure the measures of the sun, gathering together canons,
He is moved by the eternal will of the Father not for thy sake
Let alone the swift course of the moon and the progression of the
    stars,
For she runs always by the impulse of necessity.
And the progression of the stars was not brought forth for thy sake
The ethereal wide flight of birds is not veracious,
And the dissections of entrails of victims, all these are toys,
The supports of gainful cheats, fly thou these
If thou intendest to open the sacred paradise of piety,
Where virtue, wisdom, and equity are assembled
For thy vessel the beasts of the earth shall inhabit,
And the earth bewails them even to their children

DEMONS, RIII S

Nature persuades that there are pure Demons.
The bourgeons even of ill matter are profitable and good.
But these things I revolve in the recluse temples of my mind
Extending the like fire sparklingly into the spacious air,
Or fire unfigured whence a voice issuing forth,
Or light abundant, whizzing and winding about the earth
But also to see a horse more glittering than light,
Or a boy on thy shoulders riding on a horse,
Fiery or adorned with gold, or divested,
Or shooting, or standing on thy shoulders,
If thou speakest often to me thou shalt see absolutely that which
    is spoken,
For then neither appears the celestial concave bulk,
Nor do the stars shine, the light of the moon is covered,

Χθων ουκ έστηκε, βλεπεται τε παντα κεραυνοις
Μη φυσεως καλεσης αυτοπτρον αγαλμα,
Ου γαρ χρη κεινους σε βλεπειν πριν σωμα τελεσθη·
Ὁτε τας ψυχας θελγοντες αει των τελετων
　　　　απαγουσι
Εκ δ' αρα κολπων γαιης θρωσκουσι χθονιοι κυνες,
Ου ποτ' αληθες σωμα βροτῳ ανδρι δεικνυντες,
Ενεργει περι τον Ἑκατινον στροφαλον
Ονοματα βαρβαρα μηποτ' αλλαξης,
Εισι γαρ ονοματα παρ' ἑκαστοις θεοσδοτα
Δυναμιν εν τελεταις αρρητον εχοντα.
Ἡνικα βλεψης μορφης ατερ ευιερον πυρ,
Λαμπομενον σκυρτηδον όλου κατα βενθεα κοσμου,
Κλυθι πυρος φωνην

ΘΕΟΣ.

Ὁ δε θεος εστι κεφαλην εχων ἱερακος· οὑτος εστιν ὁ πρωτος αφθαρτος,
αιδιος, αγενητος, αμεσης, ανομοιοτατος, ἡνιοχος παντος καλου, αδωροδοκητος,
αγαθων αγαθατατος, φρονιμων φρονιμωτατος εστι δε και πατηρ ευνομιας
και δικαιοσυνης, αυτοδιδακτος, φυσικος, και τελειος, και σοφος, και ἱερου
φυσικου μονος εὑρετης.

The Earth stands not still, but all things appear in thunders.
Invoke not the self-conspicuous image of Nature,
For thou must not behold these before thy body is initiated:
When soothing souls they always seduce them from these
    mysteries.
Certainly out of the cavities of the Earth spring terrestrial dogs,
Which show no true sign to mortal man.
Labour about the Hecatick Strophalus
Never change barbarous names,
For there are names in every nation given from God,
Which have an unspeakable power in Rites.
When thou seest a sacred fire without form,
Shining flashingly through the depths of the World,
Hear the voice of fire.

GOD

But God is he that has the head of a hawk. He is the first
indestructible, eternal, unbegotten, indivisible, dissimilar; the
dispenser of all good; incorruptible; the best of the good, the
wisest of the wise · he is the father of equity and justice, self-
taught, physical, and perfect, and wise, and the only inventor of
the sacred philosophy.—*Euseb. Præp. Evan* lib. I. c 10

R

THE PERIPLUS

OF

HANNO.

THE PERIPLUS OF HANNO.

ΑΝΝΩΝΟΣ
ΚΑΡΧΗΔΟΝΙΩΝ ΒΑΣΙΛΕΩΣ
ΠΕΡΙΠΛΟΥΣ.

ΤΩΝ ὑπερ τας Ἡρακλεους
στηλας Λιβικων της γης μερων, ὃν και ανεθηκεν εν τῳ του
Κρονου τεμενει, δηλουντα ταδε

Ἐδοξεν Καρχηδονιοις, Ἀννανα
πλειν εξω στηλαν Ἡρακλειων,
και πολεις ντιζειν Λιβυφοινι-
κων. και επλευσεν, πεντηκον-
τορους ἑξηκοντα αγων, και
πληθος ανδραν και γυναικαν,
εις αριθμον μυριαδων τριων, και
σιτα, και την αλλην παρασ-
κευην

Ὡς δ᾽ αναχθεντες, τας
στηλας παρημειψαμεν, και
εξω πλουν δυοιν ἡμερων επλει-
σαμεν, εντισαμεν πρωτην
πολιν, ἡντινα ωνομασαμεν
Θιμιατηριον πεδιον δ᾽ αυτῃ μεγα ὑπην καπειτα προς ἑσπεραν
αναχθεντες, επι Σολοεντα Λι-
βυκον ακρωτεριον, λασιον δενδρεσι συνη θομεν, ενθαΠοσειδω-

THE VOYAGE
OF HANNO, COMMANDER OF THE
CARTHAGINIANS

ROUND the parts of Libya beyond
the Pillars of Hercules, which he
deposited in the temple of Saturn

It was decreed by the Carthaginians, that Hanno should undertake
a voyage beyond the Pillars of Hercules, and found Libyphœnician cities
He sailed accordingly with sixty ships
of fifty oars each, and a body of men
and women to the number of thirty
thousand, and provisions and other
necessaries

When we had passed the Pillars
on our voyage, and had sailed beyond
them for two days, we founded the
first city which we named Thymiaterium Below it lay an extensive
plain. Proceeding thence towards
the west, we came to Soloeis, a promontory of Libya, a place thickly
covered with trees, where we erected
a temple to Neptune , and again pro-

νος ἱερον ἰδρισαμενοι, παλιν
επεβημεν προς ἡλιον ανισχοντα
ἡμερας ἡμισυ, αχρι ελομισθη-
μεν εις λιμνην ου πορῤω της
θαλαττης κειμενην, καλαμου
μεστην πολλου ναι μεγαλου.
ενησαν δε και ελεφαντες, και
τἄλλα θηρια νεμομενα παμ-
πολλα

  Την τε λιμνην παραλ-
λαξαντες ὁσον ἡμερας πλουν,
ͺατῳκησαμεν πολεις προς τῃ
θαλαττῃ καλουμενας, Καρικον
τε τειχος, και Γυττην, και
Αγραν, και Μελιτταν, και
Αραμβꞷν. κᾳκειθεν δ᾽ αναχθεντες, ηλθομεν επι μεγαν
ποταμον Λιξον, απο της Λιϐυης
ῥεοντα. παρα δ᾽ αυτον, Νομαδες
ανθρωποι Λιξιται. βοσκηματ᾽
ενεμον, παρ᾽ οἱς εμειναμεν αχρι
τινος, φιλοι γενομενοι Τουτων
δε καθ᾽ ὑπερθεν, Αιθιοπες φκουν
αξενοι, γην νεμομενοι θηριωδη
διειλημμενην ορεσι μεγαλοις,
εξ ὧν ῥειν φασι τον Λιξον
περι δε τα ορη, κατοινειν ανθρωπους αλλοιομορφους Τρωγλο-
δυτας οὑς ταχυτερους ἱππων εν
δρομοις εφραζον οἱ Λιξιται

  Λαϐοντες δε παρ᾽ αυτων ἑρ-
μηνεας παρεπλεομεν την ερημην
προς μεσημϐριαν, δυο ἡμερας
εκειθεν δε παλιν προς ἡλιον
ανισχοντα, ἡμερας δρομον ενθα
εὑρομεν εν μυχῳ τινος κολπου,

ceeded for the space of half a day
towards the east, until we arrived at
a lake lying not far from the sea, and
filled with abundance of large reeds.
Here elephants, and a great number
of other wild beasts, were feeding

  Having passed the lake about a
day's sail, we founded cities near the
sea, called Cariconticos, and Gytte,
and Acra, and Melitta, and Arambys. Thence we came to the great
river Lixus, which flows from Libya
On its banks the Lixitæ, a shepherd
tribe, were feeding flocks, amongst
whom we continued some time on
friendly terms. Beyond the Lixitæ
dwelt the inhospitable Ethiopians,
who pasture a wild country intersected
by large mountains, from which they
say the river Lixus flows. In the
neighbourhood of the mountains lived
the Troglodytæ, men of various appearances, whom the Lixitæ described
as swifter in running than horses.

  Having procured interpreters from
them we coasted along a desert country towards the south two days.
Thence we proceeded towards the
east the course of a day. Here we
found in a recess of a certain bay

νησον μικραν, κυκλον εχουσαν
σταδιαν πεντε ην κατῳκησα-
μεν, Κερνην ονομασαντες. ετεκ-
μαιρομεθα δ' αυτην εκ του
περιπλου, και ευθυ κεισθαι
Καρχηδονος εφκει γαρ ὁ πλους,
ε/ τε Καρχηδονος, επι στηλας,
/αλειθεν επι Κερνην

Ἰουντευθεν εις λιμνην αφι-
κομεθα, διχ τι/ος ποταμου
μεγαλου διαπλευσαντες, Χρε-
της. ειχεν δε νησους ἡ λιμνη
τρεις μειζους της Κερνης αφ'
ὡν ἡμερησιον πλουν κατανυ-
σαντες, ει, την μυχον της
λιμνης ηλθομεν ὑπε, ἡν ορη
μεγιστα ὑπερετεινεν, μετα
α/θρωπων αγριαν, δερματα
θηρεια ενημμενων, οἱ πετροις
βαλλοντες, απηραξα/ ἡμας,
κωλυο/τες εκδηναι εκειθεν πλε-
οντες, εις ἑτερον ηλθομεν ποταμον μεγαν και πλατιν, γε-
μοντα /ροκοδειλων και ἱππων πο-
ταμιων ὁθεν δε παλιν αποτρεψ-
αντες, εις Κερνην επανηλθομεν

Εκειθεν δε επι μεσημβρι-
ας επλευσαμεν δωδεκα ἡμε-
ρας, την γην παραλεγομενοι
ἡ/ πασαν /ατῳκουν Αιθιοπες,
φευγοντες ἡμας, και ουχ ὑπο-
μενοντες. ασυνετα δ' εφθεγ-
γοντο, και τοις μεθ' ἡμων Λιξ-
ιταις. τη δ' ουν τελευταιᾳ
ἡμερᾳ, προσωρμισθημεν ορεσι
μεγαλοις δασεσιν. η/ δε τα των

a small island, containing a circle
of five stadia, where we settled a
colony, and called it Cerne. We
judged from our voyage that this
place lay in a direct line with Carthage, for the length of our voyage
from Carthage to the Pillars, was
equal to that from the Pillars to Cerne.

We then came to a lake which we
reached by sailing up a large river
called Chretes This lake had three
islands, larger than Cerne, from which
proceeding a day's sail, we came to
the extremity of the lake, that was
overhung by large mountains, inhabited by savage men, clothed in skins
of wild beasts, who drove us away by
throwing stones, and hindered us
from landing. Sailing thence we
came to another river, that was large
and broad, and full of crocodiles,
and river horses; whence returning
back we came again to Cerne

Thence we sailed towards the south
twelve days, coasting the shore, the
whole of which is inhabited by Ethiopians, who would not wait our approach
but fled from us Their language was
not intelligible even to the Lixitæ,
who were with us Towards the last
day we approached some large mountains covered with trees, the wood of
which was sweet-scented and varie-

WILLIAM PICKERING,
LONDON, 1828.

Thomas White, Printer,
Johnson's Court.

CPSIA information can be obtained
at www.ICGtesting.com
Printed in the USA
BVHW061453050721
610882BV00006B/14